HOUSTON GOURMET COOKS

A collection of favorite recipes from 21 of Houston's most creative restaurants

by
Ann Criswell

Foreword – Don Nelson
host of "Good Morning Houston" – Channel 13
Illustrations – Ken Boehnert

Publisher – Fran Fauntleroy

Acknowledgments

Foreword by Don Nelson
Host of "Good Morning Houston," Channel 13

Cover and illustrations – Ken Boehnert

Back cover photograph – George Gomes

Design – Larry Knapp

Tablesetting – Crate & Barrel

Flowers – Bob Galloway

Champagne – Perrier-Jouet compliments of
Chateau and Estates Wines, New York,
and Glazer's, Houston

Printing – Gulf Printing

Houston Gourmet Cooks
Houston, Texas

Printed in the United States of America

ISBN 0-9613643-3-5

★

*Dedicated
to all those who appreciate
the finer tastes in life.*

★

Contents ★★★

Foreword by Don Nelson 8
Introduction 9

Backstreet Cafe 10-13
Salmon Mousse Mold
Seafood Gumbo
Grilled Chicken Sandwich
Honey Mustard Dressing
Chicken-Broccoli Salad
Carrot Cake
Chocolate Amaretto Cheesecake

Bayou City Oyster Company 14-17
Snapper Royale
Seafood Casserole
Chicken Dick
Divinity Shrimp
Lemon Potatoes
Lemon Ice Cream

Brennan's 18-23
Redfish Fritters with Jalapeno Tartar Sauce
Crawfish Enchiladas with Green Chili Salsa
Trout with Roasted Pecans and
   Creole Meuniere Sauce
Lamb Chili
Creole Bread Pudding Souffle
   with Whiskey Sauce

Damian's Cucina Italiana 24-29
Damian's Caponata
Tortellini in Brodo
Arugula Salad With Stuffed Peppers
Josef's Chicken Salad
Snapper Russo
Zucchini "Il Mulino"
Oranges Marissa

Lancaster Grille 30-33
Cream of Onion Soup The Lancaster
Crab Royal With House Dressing
Bibb and Stilton Salad
Poached Salmon With Green Sauce
Tournedos a la Maison
White Chocolate Mousse

Lantern Inn 34-37
Saute Crabmeat Marlene
Breast of Cornish Hen
Creamed Romaine Lettuce
Steak Diane for Two
Fish Milano Flambe
Chocolate Dutchman Flambe

La Reserve, Inn on the Park 38-41
Wild Mushroom Raviolis With Chive Sauce
Zucchini Bisque With Crabmeat
Beef Tenderloin With Two Sauces
Lamb Loin With Spinach Cakes
Meringue Tartlettes With Raspberries

La Tour d'Argent 42-45
Noix de Saint Jacques Provencale
   (Scallops Provencale)
Salade Panachee a l'Huile d'Olive (Mixed
   Lettuce Salad With Olive Oil Vinaigrette)
Soupe de Legumes aux Fruits de Mer
   (Clear Vegetable Soup With Seafood)
Noisettes d'Agneau au Basilic
   (Lamb Medallions With Basil Sauce)
Champignons Sautes au Beurre D'Ail
   (Mushrooms Sauteed With Garlic Butter)
Tarte Chaude aux Pommes Sauce Abricot
   (Hot Apple Tart With Apricot Sauce)

Magnolia Bar & Grill 46-49
Crawfish Bisque
Crawfish Etouffee
Magnolia Salad
Seafood-Stuffed Eggplant
Baked Duck With Rice Dressing
White Chocolate Mousse

Montesano Ristorante Italiano 50-55
Delicatezza Della Spangna
   (Red Spanish Shrimp Sauteed in Wine)
Eggplant Della Mamma
   (Eggplant Mama's Style)
Crostini di Fontina
   (Fried Sandwich Appetizer)
Cotoletta Milanese (Veal Cutlet Milanese)
Perciatelli al Fuoco di Roma
   (Perciatelli Pasta Roma)
Tiramisu

Nash D'Amico's Pasta & Clam Bar . 56-59
Fried Squid (calamari)
Steamed Mussels
New England Clam Chowder
Spinach Pasta
Marinara Sauce
Chicken Parmesan
House Salad

Ninfa's 60-63
Ninfa's Green Sauce
Fajitas with Marinated Onions
Pico de Gallo
Refried Beans
Mexican Rice
Pina Teocali
  (Pineapple-Coconut Ice Cream Dessert)

Oak'n Bucket 64-67
Hot Cakes
Cheese Soup
Breast of Chicken
Fried Mushrooms With Horseradish Sauce
French Silk Pie

Ouisie's 68-73
Grilled Tuna Ouisie With Gremalotta
Shrimp Acapulco
Stuffed Pork Tender
Garlic Mashed Potatoes
Vegetarian Variation #1 on Lemon Ginger Rice
Roasted Red Bell Peppers With
  Bacon and Cheese Sandwich
Negre en Chemise

Peng's 74-77
General Tso's Chicken
Peng's Special Beef
Eggplant in Garlic Sauce
Fried Noodles with 10 Ingredients

Rotisserie for Beef and Bird 78-81
Bisque of Butternut Squash and Apples
Linguine and Fresh Seafood in a Spicy Sauce
Grilled Shrimp and Chicken on Brochette
Medallions of Veal with Julienne of
  Vegetables and Cheese
Poached Fresh Pears with Zabaglione Sauce

Ruggles Grille 82-85
Snapper and Crab Chowder
Black Pepper Pasta with
  Sweet Garlic Cream and Chicken
Warm Grilled Chicken Salad with
  Roquefort and Walnuts
Grilled Red Snapper with Spicy Crawfish Salsa
Blanca's Strawberry Cream Roll

San Carlos 86-89
Sopes (appetizers)
Tortilla Soup
Chilaquiles (baked casserole of chicken,
  chilies and cheese)
Snapper Veracruzana
Mango Mousse

Sausalito 90-93
Bammel Garden Salad with Goat Cheese
Ceviche Sausalito
Fettucine Dino
Redfish Aldo
Chicken a la Grecque
Domenico's Cheesecake

Taste of Texas 94-97
Tortilla Soup
Mushrooms in Butter
Butter Sauce for Sizzling Steaks
Taste of Texas Cornbread
Cinnamon Slammer
Cinnamon Coffee

Tila's 98-101
Gazpacho
Spicy Blue Cornmeal Gulf Shrimp
  with Cold Marinated Tomatoes
Chicken Torta Sandwich
Refried Black Beans
Sauteed Bananas Flamed in Dark Rum

Special Helps 103-105
Shopping Guide 106
Index 107-110
About Ann Criswell 111
Who's Who Houston Gourmet Cooks . 112

Foreword

by Don Nelson

For twelve years I've been observing the changing food scene on local talk show cooking segments. I've also been able to wander behind closed doors of local restaurants watching changes take place in everything from basic bulk beef bistros to unending multicultural seafood houses.

During the same time, my book case has been filling up with more than 500 palate-pleasing publications ranging from quick-and-easy reindeer meatballs to fun things to do with outdated Velveeta.

This newest Ann Criswell collection further illustrates how far we've come in the food world in Houston. As to be expected, this ongoing pleasing presentation of our favorite foods by top local restaurants has inspired their patrons to recreate certain dishes themselves at home.

Nothing beats first hand information on cooking, especially when it has been translated and filtered properly, removing any words that Escoffier couldn't spell himself. It took me years to realize that gourmet wasn't Steve and Eydie's last name, that a sous chef wasn't an Indian cook from North Dakota, that haute cuisine wasn't a cafe in Indiana . . .

After giving the food business some serious thought, I've decided that it is you, the home cook, who has set the trends and maintained certain traditions that your favorite restaurants have practiced. Over the years you've asked for less fried and more fresh; you've been willing to try wild and outrageous blends of spices and sauces. Licking your lips and loving it, you've allowed your local eatery to take your taste buds around the world and back, stopping in a small Texas town or two for a few of "Mama's Specials."

Now, after all your requests have been met, you find yourself wanting to prepare the dishes yourself. So here is a wonderful selection of recipes from some of Houston's most respected restaurants. "Houston Gourmet Cooks" will absolutely thrill those who enjoy a rush of creativity now and again in the kitchen.

You'll discover that our young restaurateurs and chefs believe in simplicity and good nutrition and that they place a strong emphasis on eye appeal and presentation.

One thing I've discovered from watching chefs perform all these years is that a master-piece need not be complicated. Now you will be able to duplicate these dishes in your own kitchen without complicated or expensive equipment. You will also learn that your favorite spices and other ingredients are readily available in our local supermarkets.

Houston food does have its own identity, one you will recognize and enjoy sharing with your friends. I have both of Ann Criswell's previous collections of Houston restaurant recipes and they are both worn thin from use. Now I guess I'll have 501 cookbooks, because this is a must for anyone!

Introduction

After a particularly satisfying meal at your favorite restaurant, haven't you often said to yourself, "I wish I knew how to make that at home." Or have you tried to duplicate a favorite restaurant dish and learned what a project it is to make something that a chef does so effortlessly?

If you identify with either of the above experiences you'll welcome this book. In "Houston Gourmet Cooks" 21 of Houston's most creative restaurant owners and chefs share recipes for many of their favorite signature dishes.

Some of the recipes are unbelievably simple; others may present more of a challenge, but all can be accomplished with practice. They should all provide some fun in the kitchen and give you a greater appreciation of the restaurants' philosophies and influence on our lifestyle.

Today Houstonians have an opportunity to enjoy some of the most exciting food being produced in America, in a variety of fascinating settings.

Whether it is simple food rooted in Texas' history—corn, wild game, beef, fresh fruits and vegetables—or exotic new arrivals from foreign shores, Houston restaurants are wonderfully inventive.

It wasn't always thus. As an observer of the restaurant scene during the past 21 years as food editor of the Houston Chronicle, I am constantly amazed at the culinary evolution— or revolution—especially in lighter, more health-conscious foods.

Twenty-one years ago, Houston was a shrimp cocktail, beef and bourbon-and-branch water town. There was no liquor-by-the-drink law, and one of my favorite recollections is of Houstonians in their formal black tie best trooping into the likes of the Shamrock Hilton ballroom, carrying the evening's supply of liquor in a brown paper bag.

More worldly fare has since worked its way into our menus—and our affections, and many of our chefs and restaurants have earned reputations far beyond our regional boundaries. We owe them a debt of gratitude for expanding our culinary horizons.

They have introduced us to a palate-staggering array of choices and tastes— American, Texan, Southwestern, Southern, Cajun and Creole, Mexican, Chinese, Thai, Vietnamese, Korean, Indian, Japanese, Philippine, Greek, Lebanese, Armenian, Caribbean, Moroccan.

What fun to savor these enticing flavors and perhaps combine them with cherished traditional foods or incorporate them into more contemporary menus.

Enjoy the changing taste of Houston.

—ANN CRISWELL

Backstreet Cafe

FAVORITES

Salmon Mousse Mold
Seafood Gumbo
Grilled Chicken Sandwich
Honey Mustard Dressing
Chicken-Broccoli Salad
Carrot Cake
Chocolate Amaretto Cheesecake

With its sidewalk cafe ambiance, Backstreet Cafe is taking shape as a lighthearted American bistro. Owner Tracy Lee Vaught, a geophysicist at Conoco who "dropped out" in the early days of the oil decline in Houston in the early '80s, decided she would like to open a restaurant. After searching for months she found an old two-story house with a showy camphor tree in back on the S. Shepherd curve just south of Allen Parkway.

With the help of her uncle, Jack Blalock, who has traveled extensively, she has turned it into a European-style cafe with a fountain patio, flowers, deck terraces, paintings, dark wood bar and flower print wallpaper. They bought the five-seat bar from a restaurant in College Station and a friend of Tracy's, Craig Dixon, extended it and built a back bar to match.

Vaught says she wants Backstreet to be the kind of place people like to come to two or three times a week, so she planned an eclectic menu that offers a variety of comfortable, everyday foods. They include such signature dishes as a Tex-Mex style Nine Layer Dip, Baby Bakers (new potatoes stuffed with cheese, bacon, sour cream and chives), gumbo (Vaught's version of a family recipe), burgers, chicken dishes, combination sandwiches, cheesecakes, carrot cake and banana pudding.

Star Attractions

★ Patio, upper terrace and private rooms that offer pleasant settings for weddings, receptions and parties.

★ Casual atmosphere and open-air dining at umbrella tables in the midst of flowers and fountains.

★ Home-style cooking. Everything is made in-house except the bread.

Salmon Mousse Mold

2 envelopes unflavored gelatin
¼ cup cold water
½ cup boiling water
¾ cup mayonnaise
2 tablespoons lemon juice
2 tablespoons finely grated onion
1 teaspoon bottled liquid hot red pepper sauce
½ teaspoon paprika
1 teaspoon salt
2 tablespoons fresh chopped dill
3 cups salmon (fresh-poached or canned), boned and skinned
2 cups whipping cream
Garnishes

Soften gelatin in cold water. Add boiling water and stir until gelatin is dissolved. Cool.

Whisk in mayonnaise, lemon juice, onion, hot pepper sauce, paprika, salt and dill. Chill in refrigerator until somewhat thickened, but not firm.

Fold in salmon. Whip cream until stiff; fold into salmon mixture.

Pour into greased 1-quart fish-shaped mold (or mold sprayed with non-stick spray) and refrigerate until set, at least 4 hours.

To unmold: Dip mold into warm water until loosened enough at the sides that it can be turned out onto a serving dish.

Decorate with a slice of stuffed olive for the eye, a sliver of pimiento for mouth and, if desired, paper-thin slices of cucumber or radish for the scales, starting at the tail.

Serve with cocktail-size garlic toasts and black bread slices.

Backstreet Cafe Seafood Gumbo

1½ cups vegetable oil
1½ to 2 cups flour
2 cups chopped onion
1 cup chopped green bell pepper
1 cup chopped celery
1½ tablespoons pressed garlic (about 3 cloves)
2 quarts seafood or fish stock
2½ cups sliced okra (saute in a little oil to prevent stringiness)
1 to 2 bay leaves
1 teaspoon salt
½ teaspoon white pepper
½ teaspoon black pepper
½ teaspoon red pepper (cayenne)
¾ teaspoon ground thyme
½ teaspoon ground oregano
1 pound (36- to 42-count) shrimp, peeled and deveined
1¼ pounds fish such as pollock or cod

Make a roux: Heat oil until it is just at the point of smoking. Gradually whisk in flour and whisk constantly to avoid burning until the mixture turns dark brown. The darker the roux, the richer the taste. Do not let burn.

Add chopped onion, green pepper and celery a little at a time and continue stirring while it cooks. Stir in garlic and remove from heat.

Add mixture to seafood stock, a little at a time, stirring constantly. Add okra, bay leaf, salt, pepper, thyme and oregano.

Simmer until okra is tender, about 10 to 15 minutes. Add shrimp and fish. Cook 2 minutes.

To make seafood stock: Add all shrimp hulls to 2 quarts water and simmer 30 to 45 minutes over medium heat.

Grilled Chicken Sandwich for One

1   (6- or 7-ounce) chicken breast, boned and skinned
      Marinade
¼   cup melted butter
1   (5-inch) whole-wheat bun
      Honey Mustard Dressing (recipe follows)
2   slices Swiss cheese
      Tomato slices
      Purple onion rings
      Leaf lettuce

To make marinade: Use the proportions of one-third pineapple juice to two-thirds bottled teriyaki sauce, such as ⅓ cup pineapple juice and ⅔ cup teriyaki sauce for one or two chicken breasts.

Marinate chicken breast at least 2 or 3 hours. Prepare grill. Brush chicken breast with butter and grill until cooked through. (Or broil in oven.) Meanwhile, brush bun with butter and toast on grill.

To assemble: Spread Honey Mustard Dressing on both sides of bun. Layer chicken breast, Swiss cheese slices, tomato slices and onion rings; top with leaf lettuce and top of bun.

Honey Mustard Dressing

At Backstreet, this is also served with their spinach and grilled chicken salad and green salads.

4   ounces plain non-fat yogurt
5   ounces real mayonnaise
3   ounces Dijon mustard
2   ounces honey

Combine all incredients and mix well. Taste and adjust proportions as desired.

Chicken Broccoli Salad Backstreet

2   cups cooked chicken, cut in chunks
4   cups parboiled broccoli flowerettes
⅓   cup slivered almonds
⅓   cup mayonnaise
⅓   cup sour cream
⅓   teaspoon ground ginger
      Salt and pepper to taste

Mix all ingredients and refrigerate 2 hours to let flavors blend.

Notes: To cook broccoli, drop into a small amount of boiling water and cook only until crisp-tender, about 5 minutes.

Or, microwave broccoli florets and ¼ cup water at high power until crisp-tender, about 2 or 3 minutes.

To cook chicken: boil, bake or microwave.

To microwave: Place chicken in microwave dish, cover with plastic wrap and microwave on high 2 to 4 minutes, depending on size of breast and wattage of microwave.

Diet Alert: Skin chicken before boiling or baking. Use only ¼ cup slivered almonds. Substitute light mayonnaise for mayonnaise and ⅓ cup plain non-fat yogurt for sour cream.

Carrot Cake Backstreet

2 cups sugar
1½ cups vegetable oil
4 large eggs
2 cups unbleached all-purpose flour
1 teaspoon baking powder
1 teaspoon soda
1 teaspoon cinnamon
1 teaspoon salt
2 cups grated raw carrots
½ cup finely chopped walnuts

Preheat oven to 350 degrees. Grease and flour a 13x9x2-inch pan or 2 (8-inch) layer pans. Blend sugar and oil in food processor. Add eggs, one at a time, and blend well.

Sift combined flour, baking powder, soda, cinnamon and salt. Add to egg mixture while blending. Stir in carrots and walnuts by hand.

Pour mixture evenly into pans and bake at 350 degrees until cake tests done, when tester inserted in center comes out clean. Let cake cool. Frost sheet cake in pan or remove layers from pan, cool completely and frost.

Carrot Cake Frosting
1 (1-pound) box powdered sugar
½ cup butter, softened
8 ounces cream cheese, softened
1 (8-ounce) can crushed pineapple in juice, drained
¼ cup chopped walnuts
¼ cup shredded coconut

Blend powdered sugar into butter gradually, smooth. Blend in cream cheese and beat until smooth. Stir in drained pineapple, walnuts and coconut. Spread on cooled cake.

Hints: Soften butter and cream cheese in microwave on low power (do not let melt).

Chocolate Amaretto Cheesecake Backstreet

Crust
4 tablespoons butter, melted
1¼ cups vanilla wafer crumbs

Mix melted butter with crumbs. Press into the bottom of an 8- or 9-inch springform pan. Bake 8 minutes at 350 degrees. Let cool.

Filling
8 ounces semisweet chocolate
2 (8-ounce) packages cream cheese, softened
3 large eggs
1⅓ cups sugar
1 cup sour cream
½ teaspoon cinnamon
½ teaspoon almond extract
2 tablespoons amaretto liqueur
  Whipped cream
  Toasted sliced almonds

Melt chocolate over hot water in a double boiler, or melt in the microwave. Add softened cream cheese and melt until soft.

Transfer to food processor and process until smooth, adding eggs and sugar while motor is running. Add sour cream, cinnamon, almond extract and amaretto; process until smooth.

Pour into prepared crust and bake 50 to 60 minutes at 350 degrees. Center should jiggle slightly. Remove from oven. Run a knife around edges to release cake from sides.

Chill at least 2 hours. To serve: Top each slice with whipped cream and toasted sliced almonds.

Diet Alert: Substitute light cream cheese for regular, reduce sugar to 1 cup and substitute 1 cup plain non-fat yogurt for sour cream.

Backstreet Cafe
1103 S. Shepherd
Houston 77019
521-2239

Bayou City Oyster Company

Bayou City is known for its fish and seafood such as Blackened Redfish, Paradise Shrimp and gumbo, and for a unique specialty, Chicken Dick. It is named for Dick Graves, a former chairman of the poultry committee for the Houston Livestock Show and Rodeo, and the zesty seasoning may remind you of Buffalo, New York's famous Buffalo Chicken Wings.

Other dishes that keep fans coming back for more are the Cajun red beans and rice with sausage, lemon potatoes and whatever ice cream Tom Lile happens to be in the kitchen making today.

FAVORITES

Snapper Royale
Seafood Casserole
Chicken Dick
Divinity Shrimp
Lemon Potatoes
Lemon Ice Cream

I f there were a "recipe" for Bayou City Oyster Company it would call for one spoon each of Cajun and Creole cooking, one spoon of Tex-Mex and a dash of pure Texan creativity—the mixture cooks up to a big helping of fun.

Bayou City opened five years ago and is evolving into a dining complex. On one side is a more intimate little restaurant called Georgia's (after owner Tom Lile's wife); it's all done up with eggplant-colored walls, antique furniture and Tiffany chandeliers. On the opposite side is a casual patio bar with a Tex-Mex ambiance. In between is the main restaurant with a Cajun flair—friendly bar, light-toned woods and the Happy Jazz piano, a decorative center strip of tile floor whose black and white tiles are laid out like a real piano keyboard.

Star Attractions

★ Varied settings to suit varied moods.

★ Cajun specialties such as boudin sausage and catfish.

★ Fast Break Buffet timed to get you to the Rockets' professional basketball games in the nearby Summit Arena.

★ Sunday brunch.

★ Soft bread sticks (a variation of a family recipe for yeast rolls).

★ Fish prepared any way you like it—broiled, fried, mesquite-grilled or blackened.

★ Homemade ice creams.

★ Piano player in Georgia's Tuesday through Saturday nights and Sunday brunch.

Snapper Royale

3 tablespoons oil
3 eggs
14 (26 to 30-count) shrimp
3 cloves garlic
4 tablespoons butter or margarine
Flour
2 cups heavy (whipping) cream
Salt and white pepper to taste
White wine
4 (8-ounce) fillets red snapper
8 ounces lump crabmeat
Fresh parsley
Lemon cartwheels for garnish

Make an egg wash by mixing oil and beaten eggs; set aside. Chop 6 shrimp and garlic cloves and set aside.

In a separate pan make a light roux: Melt butter and whisk in as much flour as needed, 2 to 3 tablespoons. Continue stirring constantly until a light roux is achieved.

In a 2- or 3-quart saucepan, combine cream, minced raw shrimp and garlic. Bring to a light boil, add salt and pepper to taste and let cook until reduced somewhat.

Stir in roux and simmer until thickened to desired sauce consistency. Stir in a splash of white wine. Set aside and keep warm.

Dip snapper fillets in egg mixture. Melt a little butter on a flat grill or in saute pan and cook fillets 3 to 4 minutes on each side. Meanwhile, peel, devein and butterfly remaining 8 shrimp. Broil in butter to which a little garlic has been added.

Place each fillet on a plate and nap with sauce. Top with 2 ounces crabmeat and 2 broiled shrimp. Garnish with lemon cartwheels and parsley if desired.

Serves 4.

Diet Alert: Brush fillets lightly with oil, and for egg wash use only 2 whole eggs beaten with 2 egg whites instead of 3 eggs. Substitute soft tub margarine for butter, and milk or evaporated skim milk for cream.

Seafood Casserole

4 (4-ounce) lobster tails, cut in halves, but leave in shells
16 medium shrimp, peeled
16 medium size sea scallops
4 (4-ounce) snapper fillets, cut in pieces
1 pound butter
2 ounces fresh chopped garlic
Juice of 5 lemons
2 teaspoons chopped fresh parsley

Divide lobster tails, shrimp, scallops and fish fillets among 4 individual casserole dishes. Make garlic-lemon butter: Melt butter and mix with garlic, lemon juice and parsley. Simmer 3 minutes, but do not let butter brown or burn.

Pour butter mixture over seafood until about 1 inch deep in casserole. Bake 9 to 11 minutes at 350 degrees.

Serves 4.

Diet Alert: Substitute soft tub diet margarine for butter or use only ½ pound.

Chicken Dick

2 pounds boneless, skinned chicken breast, cut into 2x1-inch strips
Flour
3 eggs
3 cups evaporated milk
Melted butter
Bottled Cajun Chef hot sauce

Dip chicken strips into flour, into egg wash made by combining beaten eggs and evaporated milk, then in flour again.

Heat oil to 350 degrees in deep fryer or large, heavy skillet. Fry chicken just until golden brown, about 3 minutes. Drain on paper towels.

Place chicken in 1-quart mixing bowl; squirt with enough melted butter to lightly cover. Flip chicken gently to coat evenly.

Repeat process with hot sauce, turning to coat evenly. Serve with Blue Cheese Dressing and celery sticks.

Serves 4.

Diet Alert: Substitute 2 eggs and 2 egg whites for 3 whole eggs, evaporated skim milk for evaporated milk and diet margarine for butter. Be sure oil stays at 350 degrees while chicken is frying and drain well.

Divinity Shrimp

1 quart sour cream
2 teaspoons paprika
1 teaspoon cayenne pepper
½ teaspoon white pepper
8 ounces sliced fresh mushrooms
1 green onion, coarsely chopped
¼ pound butter
1 pound (26- to 30-count) shrimp, peeled and deveined
2 cups cooked hot rice
Lemon and parsley for garnish

Heat sour cream slightly in 1-quart saucepan (do not let boil or it will separate). Stir in spices.

In skillet, saute mushrooms and green onion in a little butter until lightly cooked. Combine with sour cream. Saute shrimp in remaining butter until pink and tender. Serve sauce over rice and top with the sauteed shrimp. Garnish with lemon and parsley.

Serves 4.

Diet Alert: Reduce sour cream to 1 cup or substitute plain non-fat yogurt. Reduce butter to ¼ cup or use soft tub diet margarine to saute shrimp and add mushrooms and green onion. Stir in sour cream or yogurt and seasonings and cook gently a few minutes; do not let boil. Serve over rice.

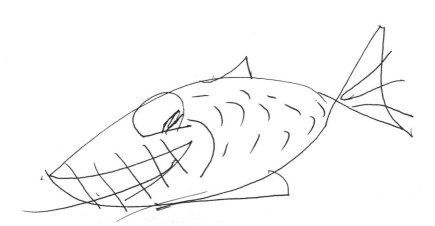

Lemon Potatoes

6   potatoes, peeled, cut in chunks
1   cup sour cream
3   teaspoons fresh lemon juice
    Grated rind of ¼ lemon
1   teaspoon chopped fresh parsley
    Salt and white pepper to taste

Cook potatoes covered in 1 inch boiling salted water until tender, about 20 to 25 minutes. Drain. Add sour cream, lemon juice and rind, parsley, salt and pepper.

Serves 8.

To cook potatoes in microwave: Place in microwave casserole, add ½ teaspoon salt and water about 1 inch deep. Cover tightly and microwave 6 minutes. Stir. Re-cover and microwave until done tender-firm, about 5 to 8 minutes longer.

Diet Alert: Substitute plain non-fat yogurt for sour cream.

Lemon Ice Cream

2   cups milk
1   heaping cup sugar
6   egg yolks
1   cup heavy (whipping) cream
2   lemons (juice and zest of peel)

Place milk and half the sugar in saucepan and bring to a boil. Remove from heat and let stand 10 to 15 minutes.

Place egg yolks and remaining sugar in electric mixer bowl and beat until they are light colored and form ribbon-like strands.

Return milk-sugar mixture to heat and bring back to a boil.

Make a custard: Off heat, pour ½ cup of the hot milk into the egg yolk mixture, whisking constantly.

Return pan to low heat and whisk egg yolk mixture into milk-sugar mixture, stirring constantly while heating mixture to 185 degrees on a candy thermometer. Do not let boil. When custard reaches 185 degrees, remove from heat and continue stirring 2 to 3 minutes more before cooling.

Pour the cooked custard into a clean bowl. Add cream, stirring to mix completely. Chill custard completely before pouring into ice cream maker.

To speed chilling, place bowl in a larger bowl containing ice water, and stir custard as it cools. When it feels cold to the touch, pour into ice cream maker.

Freeze according to manufacturer's directions. After custard has been in ice cream maker about 12 minutes, stir in lemon juice and zest to taste.

Note: This is a very versatile recipe. You can use almost any favorite flavorings. For vanilla bean ice cream, split a vanilla bean and add to milk when it is cooked with sugar. Remove vanilla bean when milk is combined with egg yolks and sugar.

Makes 1 quart.

Bayou City Oyster Company
2171 Richmond
Houston 77006
523-6640

Brennan's

FAVORITES

Redfish Fritters with Jalapeno Tartar Sauce

Crawfish Enchiladas with Green Chili Salsa

*Trout with Roasted Pecans and
Creole Meuniere Sauce*

Lamb Chili

*Creole Bread Pudding Souffle
with Whiskey Sauce*

Although its tradition is classic New Orleans cooking, Brennan's seems new every time you dine there.

The current generation of the Brennan restaurant family, cousins Alex Brennan-Martin and Dick Brennan Jr., and chef Rex Hale have woven the classics into the fabric of such "today" menu items as trout with roasted pecans, mesquite-grilled rabbit, venison hash with wild mushrooms and redfish fritters with jalapeno tartar sauce. They call it Texas Creole cuisine.

Most customers never lose their taste for Brennan's originals such as Bananas Foster, Salad Jill Jackson and Veal Chop Tchoupitoulas, but who can resist these electric new tastes?

Houstonians know Brennan's as a place for champagne occasions. During the past 20 years, the fountain patio and Garden Room have been the setting for innumerable engagement parties, weddings, wedding receptions and anniversaries.

Brennan's also is "the" place for weekend fun at the Saturday Jazz Brunch with Dixieland band, or quieter Sunday brunch, or for celebrating New Year's or the Super Bowl.

Star Attractions

★ Texas Creole cooking—the best traditional regional ingredients used in creative new ways.

★ Romantic atmosphere—shady patio with fountain, flowers, hanging baskets and twinkle lights in the trees.

★ Creative interiors by Alex's wife, Chris Brennan-Martin. She hand-placed the taupe and pink Portuguese marble tiles, and with artist Jane Bazinet hand-painted canvas for wall coverings and flat Roman shades to match the marble. Complementary paintings were personally selected by Adelaide Brennan.

★ Noteworthy building (one-time home of the Houston Junior League). It was designed by John Staub, the renowned architect of Houston's posh River Oaks section.

★ LiteStyle Cuisine, menus approved by the Diet Center. Creative low-calorie dishes such as Smoked Chicken Gumbo, Chilled Poached Spicy Oranges and Chilled Grilled Shrimp and Peppers.

★ Dramatic Combination—Dinner at Brennan's and tickets for a performance at the Alley Theatre for the price of the meal alone.

★ One of the city's best wine lists—strong on California wines, Bordeaux and Burgundies.

★ Dessert menu featuring Brennan's strawberry shortcake, Mile High Mud Pie, Creme Brulee and Creole Bread Pudding Souffle, hand-made ice creams, dessert wines, Cognacs, coffees and liqueurs. Complimentary pralines.

★ Fresh herbs from a kitchen garden (where executive chef Rex Hale and other staff members grow herbs including mint for Brennan's unique marinated mint juleps).

Redfish Fritters with Jalapeno Tartar Sauce

2 pounds redfish, cut into strips
  Louisiana hot sauce
2 cups all-purpose flour
1 teaspoon cayenne pepper
1 teaspoon black pepper
1 teaspoon salt
2 teaspoons baking powder
½ cup soy sauce
3 eggs, lightly beaten
1 cup beer
  Oil for deep-frying

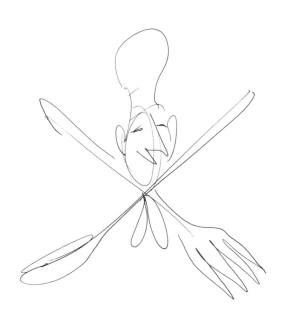

Marinate redfish in hot sauce at least 8 hours. Combine flour, pepper, salt and baking powder in large bowl.

Add soy sauce, eggs and beer. Mix thoroughly. Heat oil to 350 degrees. Dredge redfish strips in batter.

Deep-fry in 350-degree oil until fritters float. Remove from oil with slotted spoon.

Spoon Jalapeno Tartar Sauce on plates and top with fritters.

Makes 8 servings.

Jalapeno Tartar Sauce
1 cup chopped yellow onion
1 cup mayonnaise
½ cup sweet pickle relish
  Juice of 1 lemon
3 dashes bottled liquid hot red pepper sauce
  Pinch each of salt, black and red pepper

Combine all ingredients. Refrigerate if not used immediately.

Crawfish Enchiladas

¼   cup diced yellow onion
½   medium size red bell pepper, diced
½   medium size green bell pepper, diced
½   medium poblano pepper, diced
2   tablespoons corn oil
1   teaspoon minced garlic
1   Roma tomato, diced
12   ounces crawfish tails, cooked and peeled
1   tablespoon fresh cilantro, chopped
1   tablespoon chopped fresh basil
½   teaspoon ground cumin (cominos)
4   ounces Swedish farmer's cheese or Mexican white cheese, grated
    Salt and cracked black pepper to taste
8   corn tortillas
    Green Chili Salsa (recipe follows)

Make crawfish stuffing: In a large skillet over medium heat, saute onion and peppers in oil until soft.

Add garlic and tomato. Cook slightly. Add crawfish tails and herbs. Cook about 3 minutes longer. Remove skillet from stove. Thoroughly stir in grated cheese. Season with salt and pepper.

Preheat oven to 350 degrees. In a non-stick skillet over medium heat, heat tortillas on both sides until warm and soft.

Fill with equal portions of crawfish stuffing and roll up. Place, seam side down, in a 1½-quart baking dish. Cover dish with aluminum foil and bake 8 minutes at 350 degrees. Remove from oven.

To serve: Place 2 enchiladas on a serving plate. Spoon Green Chili Salsa over top. Garnish as desired. At Brennan's they garnish the plate with a whole boiled crawfish and cilantro.

Serves 4.

Green Chili Salsa

10   tomatillos, roasted and seeded
1   poblano pepper, roasted and seeded
1   teaspoon chopped fresh cilantro
1   cup chicken stock
    Salt and pepper to taste

Place tomatillos, pepper, cilantro, stock, salt and pepper in heavy saucepan over medium heat and bring to a boil. Simmer 15 minutes.

Puree in food processor. Keep warm while making enchiladas.

Note: To roast poblanos, rub with oil and grill over mesquite grill. Put in bowl, cover tightly with plastic and let steam a few minutes. To prepare tomatillos, remove papery husks and cut slightly to open. Place in boiling salted water 2 minutes. Remove and drain. Put in bowl, cover tightly with plastic wrap and let steam a few minutes.

Trout with Roasted Pecans and Creole Meuniere Sauce

1   cup shelled pecans
4   tablespoons (½ stick) unsalted butter, softened
     Juice of ½ medium lemon
1   teaspoon Worcestershire sauce
2   medium eggs, lightly beaten
1   cup milk
2   teaspoons Creole Seafood Seasoning (recipe follows)
1   cup all-purpose flour
6   (6-ounce) trout fillets
½   cup clarified butter or half vegetable oil and half margarine
     Creole Meuniere Sauce (recipe follows)
     Parsley and lemon wedges for garnish

To make Pecan Butter: Spread pecans on a cookie sheet and bake in preheated 350-degree oven 10 minutes (or spread in single layer on microwave platter and microwave on high power about 4 to 5 minutes). Coarsely chop half the roasted pecans and set aside for garnish. Place remaining half in blender or food processor. Add butter, lemon juice and Worcestershire and blend to a smooth butter. Set aside.

Combine eggs and milk; beat until well blended. Set aside. Combine seafood seasoning and flour on wax paper or in pie plate. Dredge fillets in seasoned flour, coating well. Dip in egg-milk mixture, then in seasoned flour again.

Melt or heat clarified butter in large skillet over medium-high heat. Lay fillets carefully in pan and saute quickly turning only once, until crisp and golden brown on both sides, about 2 minutes per side. Remove to warm serving platter.

To serve: Put a fillet on each plate and top with a heaping tablespoon of pecan butter, coating the entire fillet. Sprinkle with a heaping tablespoon of chopped roasted pecans. Cover trout and toppings with Creole Meuniere Sauce and garnish with parsley and lemon wedges.

Creole Meuniere Sauce

2   tablespoons vegetable oil
2   tablespoons all-purpose flour
1½   cups fish stock
     Salt and freshly ground pepper to taste
8   tablespoons (1 stick) unsalted butter, cut into chunks and softened
2   tablespoons Worcestershire sauce
     Juice of 1 lemon
¼   cup chopped fresh parsley

Heat oil in heavy skillet. Remove from heat, add flour, return to heat and cook, stirring, until roux becomes medium brown in color.

Slowly whisk in stock, bring to a boil, stirring constantly, and simmer 45 minutes. Correct seasoning. There should be about 1 cup sauce.

Transfer the brown fish sauce to a 2-quart saucepan and bring back to a quick simmer.

Whisk in softened butter and Worcestershire and continue to whisk until butter is absorbed.

Add lemon juice and parsley. Whisk again briefly and remove from heat. This sauce should be used within 45 minutes of the time it is completed.

Creole Seafood Seasoning

⅓   cup salt
¼   cup granulated or powdered garlic
¼   cup freshly ground black pepper
2   tablespoons cayenne pepper
2   tablespoons thyme
2   tablespoons oregano
⅓   cup paprika
3   tablespoons granulated or powdered onion

Combine all ingredients and mix thoroughly. Pour into large glass jar and seal airtight. Keeps indefinitely. If black pepper is not to your taste, reduce the quantity by half.

Lamb Chili

⅛   cup safflower oil
2   pounds leg of lamb meat, diced
1   yellow onion, diced
1   tablespoon minced garlic
2   poblano peppers, diced
1   quart lamb stock
2   medium tomatoes, seeded and diced
1   teaspoon chopped fresh thyme
2   tablespoons chili powder
    Salt and cracked black pepper to taste
    Homemade potato chips
    Sour cream, chopped red onion and
    chives for garnish

Heat oil in a heavy-duty dutch oven on stove over medium heat and brown lamb.

Stir in onion, garlic and peppers; cook until soft. Add lamb stock. Simmer until meat is very soft and stock has reduced, about 1 hour.

Stir in tomatoes, thyme and chili powder. Cook until mixture is of a chili consistency. Season with salt and pepper.

At Brennan's the chili, which is thick like a ragout, is served on homemade potato chips and garnished with sour cream, chopped red onion and chives.

Serves 8.

Creole Bread Pudding Souffle With Whiskey Sauce

Ella Brennan created this dessert for a gala dinner at Commander's Palace in New Orleans during the second annual Symposium on American Cuisine in 1983. It has become one of their most famous signature dishes.

1½   cups granulated sugar
8   tablespoons (1 stick) butter, softened
11   eggs
1   pint (2 cups) whipping cream
     Dash of cinnamon
1   tablespoon vanilla extract
¼   cup raisins
12   (1-inch-thick) slices fresh or stale French bread
½   cup powdered sugar
     Whiskey Sauce (recipe follows)

Preheat oven to 350 degrees. In large bowl, cream 1 cup granulated sugar and butter. Add 5 beaten eggs, cream, cinnamon, vanilla and raisins; mix well.

Pour into a 9-inch square pan 1¾ inches deep. Arrange bread slices flat in egg mixture and let stand 5 minutes to soak up some of the liquid. Turn bread over and let stand 10 minutes longer. Then push bread down so that most of it is covered by the egg mixture. Do not break the bread.

Set pan in a larger pan; fill with water to within ½ inch from top. Cover with foil. Bake 45 to 50 minutes, uncovering pudding for the last 10 minutes to brown the top. When done, the custard should still be soft, not firm.

To make souffle: Set aside 2½ cups bread pudding. Preheat oven to 375 degrees. Put 6 egg yolks and remaining ½ cup granulated sugar in top of a double boiler. Whisk over simmering water until frothy and shiny. Mix yolk mixture with reserved bread pudding until smooth.

Beat egg whites until frothy. Gradually add powdered sugar, beating constantly until the resulting meringue stands in stiff peaks. Gently fold egg whites into pudding mixture.

Butter and lightly sugar a 1½-quart souffle dish. Turn souffle mixture into the dish, filling it three-quarters full. Wipe lip of dish clean. Bake 35 to 40 minutes.

To serve: Remove souffle from oven. Serve immediately with Whiskey Sauce in a separate bowl on the side.

Whiskey Sauce
1   cup sugar
1   cup whipping cream
1   cinnamon stick of a dash of ground cinnamon
1   tablespoon unsalted butter
½   teaspoon cornstarch
¼   cup water
1   tablespoon bourbon

While souffle is baking, combine sugar, cream, cinnamon and butter in saucepan.

Add the cornstarch mixed with water and cook, stirring, until sauce is clear. Remove from heat; stir in whiskey.

Brennan's
3300 Smith
Houston 77006
522-9711

Damian's Cucina Italiana

FAVORITES

Damian's Caponata
Tortellini in Brodo
Arugula Salad With Stuffed Peppers
Josef's Chicken Salad
Snapper Russo
Zucchini "Il Mulino"
Oranges Marissa

In only four years, Damian's, owned by young, but experienced restaurateur Damian Mandola, has established a reputation as one of the top Italian restaurants in Houston. A popular lunch spot, it is good enough to lure suburbanites back to the near-downtown area at night to dine.

Architect Tony Flores and interior designer Susan White have given the low-ceilinged arched dining room a soothing old-world atmosphere that's also somewhat reminiscent of a trattoria.

The hominess is further emphasized by faded colors, rustic antiques, wooden tables and chairs, starched white tablecloths and fresh flowers. A mural of a pastoral Tuscan scene by artist Joan Loewthal defines one dining area often used for special occasion dinners or gourmet groups.

A country refectory table laden with an array of antipasto dishes greets you as you enter and tells you right away that food is really the star attraction at Damian's.

Mandola sets the style and Chef Josef Rasicci, who apprenticed in Switzerland and at Lutece in New York, executes it. Damian's is known for handmade pasta, particularly tortellini and paglia e fieno (straw and hay), a two-color pasta dish. There are three preparations of red snapper including one named for Houston developer Joe Russo.

Star Attractions

★ Food that successfully combines a family, homemade quality with new-generation creativity. Many of the dishes, such as the classic tomato spaghetti sauce, sugo, have their roots in family favorites.

★ The small, cheerful bar with red lacquer and cane chairs and square-paned windows filled with plants.

★ Complimentary caponata at each table.

★ A separate dessert menu that features Oranges Marissa (named for Damian Mandola's daughter), Lemon Tart, Mandola's version of Tiramisu (the mascarpone cheese-Italian ladyfinger dessert) and a variety of Italian ices and ice creams ranging from gelato to spumone.

★ Wines by the glass and a wine list that features an excellent variety of Italian wines. The list features barolo reserves, Gattinara Monsecco, reserve Chiantis and Picolit-Venegazzu, a rare Italian dessert wine.

Damian's Caponata

½ cup olive oil
1 large onion, diced
2 cups diced celery
1 medium eggplant (with skin), diced in ¼-inch pieces
2 tablespoons tomato paste
2 large tomatoes, peeled, seeded and diced
⅓ cup red wine vinegar
1½ teaspoons sugar
1 cup water
Salt and pepper to taste
1 tablespoon capers
¼ cup each pitted black and green olives (such as Calamata olives)
2 tablespoons pine nuts (pignolia)

Heat oil in skillet until very hot. Dice onion and celery in ¼-inch pieces. Saute eggplant in hot oil. When tender, remove from pan and set aside.

Add onion and celery to pan with a little more oil if necessary. Saute until they are tender, about 5 minutes. Return eggplant to pan.

Add tomato paste, tomatoes, wine vinegar, sugar, water, salt and pepper. Cook over medium heat 5 minutes.

Remove from heat and add capers, olives and pine nuts. Chill until serving time. Serve at room temperature.

Serves 6 to 8

Zucchini Il Mulino

Damian Mandola styled this after the zucchini served at Il Mulino restaurant on Third Street in New York.

4 medium-size zucchini
Oil for deep frying
Salt and pepper
2 medium cloves garlic, peeled and chopped
1 medium shallot, chopped
10 fresh mint leaves, chopped
Pinch of dried hot red pepper flakes
¼ cup extra virgin olive oil
5 tablespoons red wine vinegar

Wash zucchini, cut off both ends and slice lengthwise ⅛-inch thick.

Heat oil in skillet. Line a sheet pan with paper towels. When oil is hot, fry zucchini slices until golden brown.

Remove zucchini and let drain on paper towels. When all zucchini is cooked and drained, transfer to a serving platter and sprinkle with salt and pepper.

Place chopped garlic and shallot in small mixing bowl. Add chopped mint and pepper flakes. Pour olive oil and vinegar over mint.

Pour this mixture over zucchini and marinate 1 hour at room temperature. Store in refrigerator, but serve at room temperature.

Serves 8.

Arugula Salad With Stuffed Peppers

2   large red bell peppers, roasted and
     peeled
8   ounces Italian sausage
2   ounces fresh goat cheese
2   ounces fresh Mozzarella cheese, grated
½   ounce ricotta salata, finely grated
2   tablespoons sundried tomatoes packed
     in olive oil, chopped
2   tablespoons toasted pine nuts (pignolia)
     Flour
2   eggs beaten with a little water
2   cups fine breadcrumbs, preferably
     homemade
     Oil
6   bunches arugula, cleaned

Cut peppers in thirds lengthwise. Crumble sausage and brown in a skillet. When cooled, mix with cheeses, tomatoes and pine nuts.

Place a heaping tablespoon of stuffing in the middle of each pepper strip. Roll up tightly.

Dredge stuffed pepper in flour, dip in egg wash and roll in breadcrumbs.

Heat enough oil to deep-fry peppers. Fry until golden brown. Toss arugula with dressing. Place a stuffed pepper strip or two atop salad and serve.

Makes 4 to 6 salads.

Note: Peppers may be prepared and refrigerated as long as a day ahead. Fry just before serving.

Dressing
¼   cup red wine vinegar
¼   cup lemon juice
1   cup extra virgin olive oil
     Salt and pepper to taste

Combine ingredients and mix well.

Josef's Chicken Salad

A specialty of Damian's chef Josef Rasicci.

2   sweet pears, peeled and diced in
     ½-inch cubes
¼   cup finely diced onion
1   rib celery, diced
½   cup Ligurian olives, pitted, rinsed and
     dried
½   cup coarsely chopped walnuts
     Mayonnaise
4   whole chicken breasts, cooked, drained,
     cooled and diced in 1-inch pieces
     Salt and pepper to taste

Combine pears, diced onion, celery, olives, walnuts and mayonnaise with chicken. Toss well. Season with salt and pepper to taste.

Serves 6 to 8

Mayonnaise
1   anchovy fillet
1   teaspoon capers
1   egg plus 1 egg yolk
¼   cup olive oil
1   tablespoon hazelnut oil
2   tablespoons fresh lemon juice
     White vinegar
2   fresh basil leaves
     Pinch of fresh oregano
     Pinch of dry powdered mustard
1   cup or less vegetable oil
     White pepper and salt

Combine anchovy and capers in food processor and process a couple of seconds. While machine is off, add eggs. Process, adding olive oil, then hazelnut oil in a thin, steady stream.

Add lemon juice and a few tablespoons of vinegar. Add herbs and dry mustard. Add vegetable oil in a thin, steady stream, stopping to taste from time to time and adding salt, white pepper and vinegar as needed. Process to thick mayonnaise consistency.

To cook chicken breasts: Simmer in lightly salted water to cover with 1 rib celery, ½ carrot and 1 small onion. Drain and let cool, then dice.

Damian's Snapper Russo

*Named for developer and Houston civic leader
Joe Russo.*

- 4 (8-ounce) red snapper fillets
   Salt and pepper
- ¼ cup good quality olive oil
- 4 cups fine breadcrumbs, preferably
   homemade
- 2 ounces unsalted chicken stock
- 2 ounces dry white wine
- ½ teaspoon finely chopped garlic
- ½ teaspoon finely chopped shallots
- 12 large sea scallops, cut in half
- 2 bell peppers (contrasting colors),
   grilled, peeled and cut into ½-inch
   wide strips
- 1 tablespoon capers, chopped
- 6 ounces cold butter

Salt and pepper fillets. Coat with olive oil
and dredge evenly in breadcrumbs. Place over
a hot charcoal grill and grill until fish is golden
brown on both sides and firm to the touch.

Meanwhile, make sauce: Place stock,
wine, garlic and shallots in saute pan with
scallops. Cook until scallops are done and
liquid is reduced, about 5 minutes in all.

When scallops are about half done, add
peppers, capers, cold butter and salt and
pepper to taste. Continue cooking until scallops
are done and sauce is a nice consistency.

To serve: Place fillets on 4 plates. Arrange
peppers and scallops over fish. Pour sauce
over all.

Serves 4.

Tortellini in Brodo

Pasta
4 cups unbleached all-purpose flour
2 eggs
¼ cup water
1 teaspoon olive oil
Pinch of salt

Make pasta by directions for your pasta maker. If making by hand, make a well in the center of the flour and gradually incorporate beaten eggs, water, oil and salt.

Work to a paste, then knead until smooth and satiny, about 10 minutes. Round up in a ball and let rest about 15 minutes. Roll pasta out in a circle on lightly floured surface by hand or on the thinnest setting on the pasta machine. Cut out circles with a 2-inch round cookie cutter. Work quickly so pasta does not dry out.

Place ¼ to ½ teaspoon stuffing in the center of each pasta circle. Moisten edges of circle with a little water and fold circle almost in half making a half-moon shape, but leaving an uneven edge. Twist the half moon around your little finger pressing the ends together and pushing the uneven edge forward to form the tortellini.

Place tortellini on a well-floured tray. If not using immediately, you can freeze for later use. Place tray in freezer until tortellini are well frozen. Remove from tray, place in plastic bags and return to the freezer.

When ready to cook, bring 1½ quarts chicken broth, preferably homemade, to a boil in a stock pot. Season with salt and pepper. Place 24 tortellini in the boiling broth and boil until they float to the top, about 2 minutes. If tortellini are frozen, boil 3 to 5 minutes.

Ladle soup into bowls, dividing tortellini evenly. Sprinkle with a little chopped fresh parsley.

Serves 6 to 8.

Note: Never thaw frozen tortellini; place them directly into boiling stock.

Tortellini Stuffing
1 bunch fresh spinach, stems removed
1 tablespoon butter
1 tablespoon finely chopped yellow onion
1 pound ricotta cheese (drain 1 hour in colander)
1½ cups freshly grated Parmesan cheese
2 egg yolks
Salt and pepper to taste
Generous pinch of freshly grated nutmeg

Wash spinach in three or four changes of cold water, then boil in a small amount of salted water about 2 minutes. Drain, squeeze dry and finely chop.

Melt butter in a skillet and add onion. Cook 2 minutes, then add spinach and saute 2 minutes more. Remove from heat; let cool.

Combine cheese, spinach and egg yolks in a bowl and mix thoroughly. Add salt, pepper and nutmeg to taste. Refrigerate stuffing until ready to use.

Oranges Marissa

Named for Damian Mandola's daughter Marissa.

8	oranges
2	large lemons
3	cups water
1⅓	cups sugar
1	cup plus 5 tablespoons dry white wine
3	tablespoons Grand Marnier liqueur

Cut a thin slice from top and bottom of each orange. Strip orange and lemon peel from fruit from top to bottom, making sure none of the white pith is on the peel.

Cut peel into thin julienne strips. With sharp knife, cut down and around each orange removing all white pith and leaving only the flesh.

Bring water to a boil. Add peel and boil 5 minutes. Drain and transfer to non-aluminum saucepan. Add sugar and 1 cup wine.

Bring to a boil over medium low heat. Increase heat and boil until syrupy and medium caramel color. Remove from heat. Stir in remaining wine and liqueur.

Place oranges on a serving platter or in shallow crystal bowl and pour sauce with rind over oranges. Marinate 1 hour. Serve at room temperature. Store in refrigerator.

Serves 8.

Damian's Cucina Italiana
3011 Smith St.
Houston 77006
522-0439

Lancaster Grille

FAVORITES

Cream of Onion Soup The Lancaster
Crab Royal With House Dressing
Bibb and Stilton Salad
Poached Salmon With Green Sauce
Tournedos a la Maison
White Chocolate Mousse

The Lancaster Grille is located in The Lancaster Hotel, a small luxury hotel in downtown Houston. The hotel's hand-picked antiques, original paintings, polished brass and mahogany paneling suggest a quiet English manor has been set down in the heart of Houston's cultural, civic and financial district.

The 64-seat grille (reservations are strongly advised) continues the English country theme with shuttered windows, hunter green walls, wooden floors and framed oils and engravings of hunting dogs and horses from the 1800s.

The menu, however, is a blend of contemporary and traditional—smoked Scottish salmon, hearts of palm salad and classic Veal Scallopine contrast with linguini with wild mushrooms and smoked Texas sausage, venison pate and a heart-healthy clear seafood soup with vegetables, herbs and wine.

Ronald L. Whitman, a certified executive chef, is responsible for the appealing combination of cooking styles, fine foods and wines and healthful cooking techniques.

The Grille's strategic location—easily accessible to the new Gus Wortham Theatre Center, Jones Hall and the Alley Theater — makes it the perfect spot to have a before- or after-theater dinner or snack or after-the-opera drink or dessert.

Star Attractions

★ Sidewalk umbrella tables where you can order an appetizer, soup or between-acts drink or have an al fresco meal while people-watching.

★ Antique-filled setting—Chippendale mirrors, George III and George IV-period rosewood, satinwood and mahogany tables and bookcases and the scent of potpourri create an elegant, genteel atmosphere. Tea is served in the afternoons in the drawing room-like ambiance of the lobby.

★ Fine food with emphasis on heart-healthy cooking. Symbols indicate heart-healthy items on menu.

★ Full breakfast menu featuring freshly squeezed juices, cheese blintzes, oatmeal, birchermuesli, granola and freshly brewed decaffeinated coffee.

★ Twenty-four hour room service available for hotel guests.

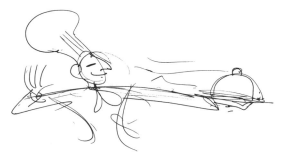

Cream of Onion Soup The Lancaster

5   cups (about 2½ pounds) minced white onion
⅙   cup (about 2 tablespoons) minced shallots
½   stick (¼ cup) unsalted butter
1   tablespoon flour
3   cups chicken stock or thinned chicken broth
½   teaspoon salt
½   teaspoon white pepper
¼   teaspoon freshly grated nutmeg
4   cups heavy (whipping) cream
6   round crusty rolls, about 6 inches in diameter and 2 to 3 inches thick (such as boule rolls)
⅛   cup Calvados (applejack)
¼   cup minced fresh parsley leaves

In a kettle cook onions and shallots in butter over moderately low heat, stirring, 15 minutes or until they are softened. Stir in the flour and cook the mixture, stirring, 2 minutes.

Add the stock, salt, pepper and nutmeg; bring the stock to a boil. Simmer the mixture, stirring occasionally, 30 minutes or until it is reduced by a third.

Add the cream and simmer again 30 minutes or until reduced by a third.

Cut the top ¼-inch from the rolls with a serrated knife, carefully remove the center of the rolls, leaving a ⅓-inch thick shell.

Place each roll on a plate or in a bowl and ladle soup into it. Add 1 teaspoon Calvados to each serving and sprinkle with parsley.

Makes about 8 cups, 4 to 6 servings.

Crab Royal

4   large firm red tomatoes
12   ounces lump crabmeat
4   ounces stemmed, washed fresh spinach leaves
     House Dressing

Wash tomatoes. On the bud end of each, make four deep cuts across the tomato cutting three-fourths of the way through to make 8 equal wedges (do not cut all the way through).

Using a melon baller or spoon, scoop out the inside of the tomato (save for sauce or soup). Rinse and drain the resulting flower.

Place a bed of one ounce finely chopped spinach leaves in the bottom of each tomato flower. Mix lump crab with ½ cup House Dressing.

On each of 4 salad plates, make a small pool of 1 teaspoon dressing. Center the stuffed tomato on the pool of dressing. Spoon equal amounts of the crab into the tomatoes. Serve well chilled.

Serves 4.

Lancaster House Dressing
2   egg yolks
¼   cup Dijon mustard
½   cup raspberry vinegar
1½   teaspoons lemon juice
1½   cups olive oil
½   cup walnut oil
½   teaspoon dried tarragon leaves (or 1½ teaspoons fresh)
½   teaspoon salt

In a mixing bowl, whip egg yolks until light yellow. Continue beating while adding the mustard, vinegar and lemon juice.

Continue beating as you add the oils very slowly in a thin stream. Add tarragon and salt and whip 2 more minutes.

Makes 3 cups.

Tournedos a la Maison

8 (3-ounce) medallions of beef tenderloin
16 large white mushrooms
1 large shallot, finely chopped
   Butter
¼ cup chicken broth
1 tablespoon aromatic bitters
¼ cup heavy (whipping) cream
8 toasted bread rounds such as French bread or sliced French rolls, cut the size of the beef medallions
1½ cups Bearnaise sauce

Stem all mushrooms. Set aside the 8 prettiest ones. Finely chop remaining mushrooms and all stems. Saute shallots in a small amount of butter. Add mushrooms when shallots are clear; saute lightly. Add chicken broth and bitters and cook until liquid is reduced by two-thirds.

Add salt and pepper to taste. Add cream and cook until the mixture thickens. Cool the mixture and stuff it into remaining stemmed mushrooms.

Grill beef to desired doneness. Toast the bread rounds. Heat mushrooms on the grill slightly.

Assemble by placing tournedo on toast round and topping with heated mushroom. Top with Bearnaise sauce. Serve two per person.

Serves 4.

Poached Salmon with Green Sauce

   Water
1 cup dry white wine
   Juice of 1 lemon
2 teaspoons chopped fresh dill
8 (8-ounce) salmon steaks
   Lime slices and fresh dill for garnish
   Green Sauce (recipe follows)

Heat enough water to cover fish to a simmer in fish poacher or roaster set over two burners. Add wine, lemon juice and chopped dill. Add salmon steaks. Return to a simmer and simmer lightly until fish flakes (do not overcook).

Remove fish from poaching liquid and place on warm serving platter. Garnish with lime slices and fresh dill. Serve with green sauce.

Serves 8.

Green Sauce
1 cup sour cream
2 tablespoons freshly grated Parmesan cheese
1 clove garlic, mashed
3 tablespoons minced watercress
2 tablespoons chopped fresh spinach leaves
1 tablespoon chopped chives
1 tablespoon chopped fresh parsley
1 tablespoon chopped fresh dill
   Salt and pepper to taste

Combine sour cream and cheese with garlic, watercress, spinach, chives, herbs and salt and pepper to taste.

Serve on the side or spoon across the edge of the salmon steaks.

Diet Alert: To reduce calories, use plain non-fat yogurt instead of sour cream.

Bibb and Stilton Salad

4 heads Bibb lettuce
½ cup pine nuts (pignolia)
1 cup Lancaster House Dressing
8 ounces Stilton cheese
1 bunch watercress

Clean lettuce and refrigerate overnight.
Toast pine nuts in a single layer on baking sheet in 300-degree oven until lightly brown in color (or toast in microwave).
In large bowl, toss the dressing and lettuce together.
Portion onto 8 salad plates. Crumble cheese over top and sprinkle with pine nuts. Garnish with watercress.

Serves 8.

The Lancaster's White Chocolate Mousse

8 ounces white chocolate
2 teaspoons butter
3 cups heavy (whipping) cream
½ cup powdered sugar
3 eggs, separated
½ teaspoon vanilla extract
1 ounce white creme de cacao liqueur

Melt chocolate with butter in a warm (150-degree) oven (or in microwave on low power; stir to smooth).
In a separate bowl, whip cream (chill cream, bowl and beaters thoroughly before beating), adding powdered sugar.
In another bowl, whip egg whites very stiff. When the chocolate is soft and mixable, whisk in egg yolks; mix well. Fold in beaten egg whites, then the whipped cream.
Add vanilla and cream de cacao and mix until smooth. Refrigerate overnight.

Serves 8.

Lancaster Grille
The Lancaster Hotel
701 Texas Ave.
Houston 77002
228-9500

Lantern Inn

FAVORITES

Saute Crabmeat Marlene
Breast of Cornish Hen
Creamed Romaine Lettuce
Steak Diane for Two
Fish Milano Flambe
Chocolate Dutchman Flambe

L antern Inn with its beautiful lead glass doors and windows, fabric-draped walls and alcoves and muted lighting is a comfortable, quiet retreat from busy Memorial Drive only a few yards away from its front door. The modest restaurant has been in the same location for 25 years and continues to deliver the quality and type of food its fans, both new and old, expect.

The restaurant excels at classics such as French onion soup, lump crabmeat cocktail, escargot, Caesar salad, stuffed flounder, chateaubriand, Steak Diane, Beef Stroganoff and Cherries Jubilee.

Tableside cooking is the specialty in the evenings, and the eclectic menu features fresh fish and seafood, fine beef and a number of flambe desserts.

Rick Pirooz, a veteran in the food and beverage business with the Fairmont in Dallas, the Hyatt-Regency hotel and other Houston restaurants, bought Lantern Inn in 1979.

He and long-time chef Dean Hudson continue to build on a strong foundation of courtesy and professionalism.

The restaurant has recently been expanded with a casual dining area called The Veranda.

The menu hasn't changed since 1982, but Pirooz hired a dietitian to revise many dishes along more healthful guidelines.

Lantern Inn is a popular place for business lunches and neighborhood gatherings, but it's a romantic spot, too.

The back booth is known as "the lovers' booth" and at least twice a month, couples get engaged there, says Pirooz. They return to celebrate anniversaries, too, he says.

Star Attractions

★ Match folders printed with the guest's name on reserved tables.

★ Each woman guest receives a rose when she leaves.

★ Complimentary pate on each table and complimentary cup of gumbo with each meal in the evenings.

★ Bread board with mini loaves of homemade whole-wheat and white bread.

★ Long-time favorites still on the menu—Sauteed Crabmeat Marlene (named for former owner Marlene Hahn), Calf's Liver Saute and the lunch time best-sellers, broiled red snapper with lemon butter sauce and Trout Almondine.

★ Hatchcovers—a dessert of strawberries, liqueurs and vanilla ice cream made only when fresh strawberries are available. Flambe desserts such as Bananas Foster and Cherries Jubilee, and a Lantern Inn exclusive, Chocolate Dutchman Flambe served in distinctive Mexican glass coupes.

★ Many items available for the health-conscious diner watching calories, cholesterol and sodium.

★ Cordial cart with selection of fine liqueurs and Cognacs.

★ The Veranda is a pleasant setting for rehearsal dinners, receptions.

Saute Crabmeat Marlene

2   cloves garlic, chopped
2   tablespoons butter
8   ounces super lump crabmeat
1   cup sliced fresh mushrooms
½   cup white wine
1   tablespoon brandy
     Worcestershire sauce, salt and pepper
     to taste
1   teaspoon chopped fresh parsley

Saute garlic in butter. Add crab and sliced mushrooms and cook 3 to 5 minutes.

Stir in wine, brandy and a dash of Worcestershire. Add salt and pepper to taste.

To serve: Top with chopped parsley and spoon over a bed of wild rice, long grain-wild rice blend or dilled rice.

Serves 1 or 2.

Diet Alert: Reduce butter to 1 tablespoon or use diet margarine. Omit salt.

Breast of Cornish Hen Lantern Inn

6   ounces boneless breast of Cornish hen
     Whole-wheat flour
2   tablespoons butter, margarine or
     vegetable oil
½   teaspoon fresh chopped parsley or
     tarragon
1   tablespoon fresh lemon juice

Dust Cornish hen breast with flour and saute in 1 tablespoon butter until desired doneness. Set aside and keep warm while preparing sauce.

Melt remaining butter and saute parsley.

Add lemon juice and stir until bubbly.

Place Cornish hen on plate and top with sauce. Serve with vegetable of your choice.

Serves 1.

Creamed Romaine Lettuce

This is a specialty at Lantern Inn and guests are always surprised to discover it's lettuce, not spinach.

16   ounces Romaine lettuce
     Butter, diet margarine or vegetable oil
2   tablespoons flour
½   cup milk (can be skim milk) or cream, warmed
½   cup chopped onion
2   cloves garlic, chopped
     Lemon juice, salt and pepper

Remove tough center ribs from lettuce, wash and shred leaves. Place wet leaves in a saucepan, cover and steam over low heat until cooked, about 10 minutes.

Meanwhile, prepare cream sauce: Melt 1 tablespoon margarine or butter in saucepan. Stir in flour with a wire whisk until a paste forms.

Pour in warm milk and whisk until smooth and thickened. Keep warm over very low heat (or in microwave) until needed.

Saute onion until golden brown. Add garlic and saute 1 to 2 minutes.

Drain lettuce in a strainer and add to onion mixture. Pour in cream sauce, season to taste with lemon juice, salt and pepper and heat through.

Serves 2 to 4.

Steak Diane for Two

1   pound beef fillet, cut in 4 pieces
2   tablespoons chopped onion
     Butter or margarine
     Salt, pepper, Worcestershire sauce, Dijon mustard
2   tablespoons brandy
2   beef bouillon cubes or 2 teaspoons beef bouillon granules, dissolved to a paste
2   chicken bouillon cubes or 2 teaspoons granules, dissolved to a paste
½   cup red wine
1   cup sliced fresh mushrooms
3   tablespoons whipping cream

Lightly saute onion in 1 teaspoon butter over medium heat.

Sprinkle salt, pepper and Worcestershire on meat; spread a little Dijon mustard on each piece.

Add meat to onion and brown to desired doneness.

Flambe with brandy (warm brandy in a ladle, pour over meat and carefully ignite with a taper match).

Stir in beef and chicken bouillon and wine. Add mushrooms and cream, stir and heat through. Garnish and serve.

Serves 2.

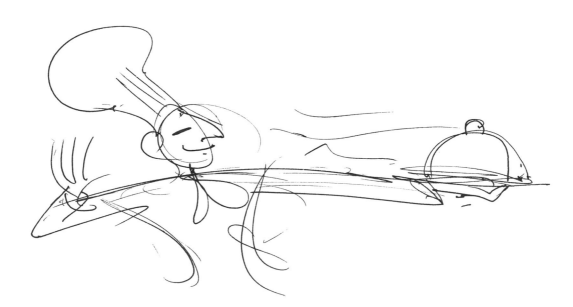

Fish Milano Flambe

2   (8-ounce) red snapper fillets
2   tablespoons water
    Paprika
½   cup chopped fresh chives
½   cup butter or soft tub margarine
2   cloves garlic, chopped
1   tablespoon chopped fresh parsley
½   cup chopped red bell pepper or tomato
4   ounces fresh lump crabmeat
    Salt and pepper
    Worcestershire sauce
2   tablespoons brandy
2   tablespoons sherry
    Chopped fresh parsley for garnish
2   lemon halves

Place fillets in shallow baking pan and add water. Sprinkle with paprika. Bake in 350-degree oven about 10 minutes (10 minutes per inch of thickness of fish).

Meanwhile, lightly saute chives in butter in skillet or chafing dish, adding garlic, parsley, tomato and crabmeat, one at a time. Stir after each addition. Add salt, pepper and Worcestershire to taste.

Warm brandy and sherry in a ladle, pour over crab mixture and carefully flambe.

Remove fish, place on a plate and top with crabmeat mixture. Garnish with parsley and a lemon half.

Serves 2.

Chocolate Dutchman Flambe

½   cup blanched sliced almonds
2   tablespoons butter, melted
½   cup chocolate syrup (they use Hershey's)
2   tablespoons Vandermint chocolate-mint liqueur
2   cups vanilla ice cream

Saute almonds in butter. Add chocolate syrup. Flambe with Vandermint liqueur and pour over ice cream.

Served in footed crystal dessert coupes or bowls.

Serves 2.

Lantern Inn
12448 Memorial Dr.
Houston 77024
465-5684

La Reserve, Inn on the Park

E legance and excellence. Those two words describe Inn on the Park hotel and its showcase restaurant, La Reserve. It is everything you expect of the ultimate dining experience plus the unexpected such as an alternative menu of health-conscious dishes and a separate menu of after-dinner specialty coffees.

The hotel dominates a 28-acre park-like setting where black swans glide over a reflecting pond. The Palm Court with its waterfalls and greenery is an oasis; who would guess thousands of cars are humming along one of Houston's busiest freeways just beyond the trees.

The atmosphere is hushed and serene but not stuffy, and luxurious but appealingly understated. It's no surprise that Inn on the Park is one of Houston's favorite settings for weddings, receptions and other special occasions.

The hotel has received national acclaim including the American Automobile Association's Five-Diamond Award and four stars from Mobil, and La Reserve has received the Travel Holiday Award three consecutive years.

Currently presiding over the kitchen is executive chef Kaspar Donier, who began his apprenticeship at 16 in Zurich. French cooking remains one of his fortes, but he has wedded French techniques to Texas regional cuisine.

"I strive to create a menu that is inventive using only the best and freshest local ingredients prepared with a French influence," Donier said.

Only after the fresh produce and fish are delivered in late afternoon does he decide on the next day's specials. One day the special might be a red bell pepper sauce for grilled breast of chicken; another day, fresh fennel in a bouillabaisse of Texas Gulf Coast seafood.

The adventurous diner, especially one who enjoys wild game, will luxuriate in the culinary excitement emanating from the La Reserve kitchen—from an appetizer terrine of partridge with foie gras and hazelnuts or mosaic of melon with smoked goose breast to an entree of axis deer medallions with spatzel and two cabbages.

Star Attractions

★ Alternative cuisine—A special menu of chef's specialties for those who wish to monitor their intake of calories, cholesterol and sodium. An appetizer and main course total less than 500 calories. The menu includes many dishes that guests order because they are delicious, not because the guests are watching calories.

★ Complimentary appetizer and hand-dipped chocolates and cookies served with dinner.

★ Wine by the glass and a selection of champagne drinks like Kir Royale made with apricot, plum and other liqueurs.

★ A separate dessert menu featuring Inn on the Park's signature dishes such as Grand Marnier Fruit Cake, Hot Apple Tart with Cinnamon Ice Cream and the Cookie Basket with Assorted Fruit and Strawberry Sauce.

★ Buffet on the Bayou—Southwestern specialties with a Cajun flair every Friday night at Cafe on the Green. Or join a happy crowd for an after-the-theater or late-night snack at the Bagel Nosh on Saturday nights or Sunday brunch in the Cafe on the Green.

★ A perfect ending to a night on the town or a romantic getaway weekend—the Viennese Dessert Table, a breathtaking array of cakes, flans, tarts and French pastries from Inn on the Park's superb pastry chefs, Fridays and Saturdays from 10 p.m. to 1 a.m.

Wild Mushroom Raviolis With Chive Sauce

Won ton wrappers are a handy and clever substitute for pasta.

 12 wonton wrappers (rounds, 3 inches in diameter)
  2 ounces shiitake mushrooms, finely sliced
  3 ounces enokie mushrooms, finely sliced
  2 ounces oyster mushrooms, finely sliced
  2 tablespoons butter, melted
    Pinch each of salt, tarragon and rosemary
  1 shallot
  ⅓ cup white wine such as Riesling
  1 cup chicken broth
  ¾ cup heavy (whipping) cream
  1 bunch fresh chives

Boil wonton wrappers, 6 at a time, like pasta in large pot of boiling water; takes only 2 or 3 minutes. Let cool.

Saute mushrooms in frying pan with butter and season with herbs. Simmer about 5 minutes until all mushroom liquid is evaporated. Remove mushrooms from pan and let cool.

Drain won tons. Place a tablespoon of mushroom mixture in the middle of each and fold all sides of the wrapper up to the middle, close to the ravioli.

Steam on a rack over a little simmering water in a covered pan or wok 3 minutes.

Place shallot and white wine in a saucepan. Let cook down until reduced by half. Add chicken stock and cream.

Let mixture reduce again by half or until desired consistency is achieved. Add chives at the last minute.

Arrange 3 raviolis on a plate and cover with sauce.

Serves 4 as an appetizer.

Zucchini Bisque With Crabmeat

1 medium onion, diced
2 tablespoons butter
3 medium zucchini, diced
1 potato, diced
5 cups chicken stock
1 sprig fresh thyme
   Pinch each of salt and pepper
2 cups heavy (whipping) cream
½ cup lump crabmeat
   Chives

Fry onion in butter until transparent. Add zucchini and potatoes; fry a few minutes.

Add stock, thyme and seasonings. Simmer 30 minutes. Transfer to blender container and blend until smooth. Return to pot.

Add cream and crabmeat. Bring to a boil. Serve. Garnish with cut chives.

Serves 4 to 6.

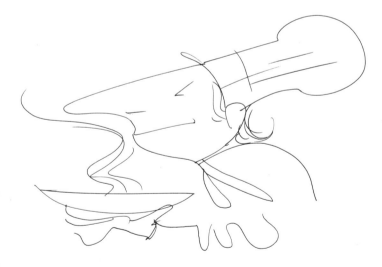

Beef Tenderloin With Two Sauces

4 beef tenderloin steaks

Grill or panfry steaks. When done, remove and keep warm. To serve: Place a portion of each sauce on plate. Arrange steak on top. Garnish with a basil leaf.

Grain Mustard Sauce
1 tablespoon chopped shallots
¾ cup Merlot wine
1 cup chicken stock
¼ cup butter
2 tablespoons grain mustard
2 sprigs fresh basil

Add shallots to pan in which steaks were cooked and saute until lightly brown.

Deglaze pan with wine and stock (pour in liquids and simmer, scraping up browned bits from bottom of pan).

Cook until reduced by half. Add small pieces of butter and whisk continuously until incorporated. Do not let boil.

When all the butter has been added, strain the sauce. Finish sauce by adding mustard and basil.

Makes enough for 4 steaks.

Horseradish Sauce
½ cup unsalted butter, softened
   Juice of 1 lemon
2 tablespoons prepared horseradish
2 tablespoons chopped chives
2 tablespoons chopped fresh parsley
   Pinch each of salt and pepper

Mix all ingredients until well combined. Season to taste.

Make a roll or pipe rosettes of butter onto a shallow pan or plate. Refrigerate until used.

Lamb Loin With Spinach Cakes

1½ pounds lamb loin
    Pinch of salt and pepper
2 tablespoons olive oil
1 shallot, chopped
1 rib celery, cut in cubes
1 small carrot, cut in cubes
    Pinch of rosemary
½ cup red wine
½ cup chicken stock

Season lamb with salt and pepper and brown it in olive oil in an ovenproof pan.

Add the shallot, celery, carrot and rosemary and roast in 375-degree oven until lamb is still pink, about 15 to 20 minutes

Remove from oven and keep in a warm place. Deglaze pan with wine and stock and simmer 5 minutes. Strain the sauce and keep warm.

Spinach Cakes
2 bunches fresh spinach
1 clove garlic, chopped
3 eggs
8 slices fresh bread (toasted and pureed to crumbs in food processor)
    Freshly grated Parmesan cheese
    Pinch each of salt, pepper and thyme
3 tablespoons olive oil

Blanch spinach (cook 30 seconds in boiling salted water). Cool immediately in ice water to preserve color. Squeeze dry; chop.

Place in a bowl and add garlic, eggs, bread crumbs and cheese. Season to taste and mix well. Spoon portions of the spinach mixture into Teflon-coated pan and flatten into rounds with the spoon. Saute cakes in oil.

Place 3 spinach cakes on each plate. Slice the lamb and place 3 lamb medallions on top of spinach cakes. Add the sauce. Garnish with a sprig of rosemary.

Serves 4.

Meringue Tartlettes With Raspberries

1 cup egg whites (about 6 large eggs)
1 cup granulated sugar
2 cups powdered sugar

Beat egg whites in electric mixer until almost stiff.

Slowly add granulated sugar and continue beating until stiff.

Gently fold in powdered sugar until well mixed. Place meringue in pastry bag with plain tube attached and pipe out 4 (4- to 6-inch) circles on a cookie sheet. Decorate borders with small circles of meringue. Bake at 200 degrees until dry, about 3 hours.

Serves 4.

Raspberry Sauce
1 (10-ounce) package frozen raspberries or 2 pints fresh raspberries and 3 ounces sugar (about ½ cup)
4 tablespoons raspberry brandy (framboise) or kirsch (clear cherry brandy)

Puree berries in blender. Strain and add sugar and a little water if necessary. Add liqueur.

Place a fresh raspberry in the middle of each meringue base.

Place meringue on center of plate and pour sauce around it. Garnish with whipped cream if desired.

La Reserve, Inn on the Park
Four Riverway
Houston 77056
871-8181

La Tour d'Argent

FAVORITES

Noix de Saint Jacques Provencale
(Scallops Provencale)
Salade Panachee a l'Huile d'Olive
(Mixed Lettuce Salad With
Olive Oil Vinaigrette)
Soupe de Legumes aux Fruits de Mer
(Clear Vegetable Soup With Seafood)
Noisettes d'Agneau au Basilic
(Lamb Medallions With Basil Sauce)
Champignons Sautes au Beurre D'Ail
(Mushrooms Sauteed With Garlic Butter)
Tarte Chaude aux Pommes Sauce Abricot
(Hot Apple Tart With Apricot Sauce)

Dining at La Tour d'Argent is a soul-satisfying and palate-pleasing experience in a unique setting—a log cabin with hunting lodge decor on the wooded banks of White Oak bayou off Loop 610.

In keeping with the hunting lodge theme, the menu often features game such as buffalo, venison and elk. One of the most popular offerings is the wild game plate which combines pheasant, duck and squab. Walls are almost concealed by hunting trophies including lion and tiger skins and more than 2,000 mounted deer antlers, moose, elk and even rhinoceros heads.

The log cabin was built in 1917 and is the oldest log cabin in Houston. It was almost destroyed by fire just as it was being readied to open as a restaurant in 1981. Lahham, his wife and friends rented a sand blaster and scraped and renovated the burned logs one by one, and the restaurant opened only slightly behind schedule.

The romantic atmosphere is enhanced by leaded glass doors and windows, stone fireplaces, wooden tongue-in-groove floors, paintings and antiques of collector quality, fine china and flowers, usually red roses, on the tables. Queen Anne reproduction chairs upholstered in burgundy leather are a recent addition. The 182 chairs were hand-carved in Italy and took three years to produce, says owner Sonny Lahham.

La Tour d'Argent is known as much for its fine French cuisine as its unique setting. It has earned the Mobil Travel Guide four-star award since 1984 and has been widely recognized for its cuisine and its exceptional wine list.

Executive Chef Dominique Dahmani is a classically trained French chef who has been working in kitchens since he was 10. He came to Houston from the Pyramid Room at the Fairmont Hotel in Dallas.

Star Attractions

★ French cuisine—one of the few traditional French restaurants in Houston.

★ Appealing setting and atmosphere for power lunches, business meetings, dinner to impress the boss or a date, or just to while away rainy hours over a bottle of wine with someone special.

★ Alcoves and rooms for secluded dining including the Garden Room which overlooks a gazebo, two man-made waterfalls and a small stream where ducks and geese glide by.

★ The resident wildlife—birds (including a cage of pigeons, doves and pheasant in the Crocodile Room), quail, raccoons, rabbits and squirrels provide a continuing floor show for diners.

★ Excellent and extensive wine list—articularly strong in French and California listings. The wine loft (available for small parties or tastings) stores 1,200 cases of wine. Wines dating to 1753 on display; drinkable vintages dating to 1898.

★ Polished, professional service.

★ Harpist plays for special occasions.

Noix de Saint Jacques Provencale (Scallops Provencale)

¾ cup clarified butter
12 ounces sea or bay scallops lightly dredged in flour
1 ounce white wine
¾ cup veal stock
2 tablespoons peeled, diced tomatoes
1 teaspoon chopped garlic
1 teaspoon chopped shallots
1 tablespoon chopped fresh parsley
3 ounces Garlic Butter (see note)
Salt and pepper

Heat a saute pan or fry pan and add clarified butter. Add scallops; cook 1 or 2 minutes on each side. Remove scallops from pan; set aside.

Add wine, stock, tomatoes, chopped garlic, shallots, parsley, garlic butter, salt and pepper to pan and cook until reduced, about 1 or 2 minutes.

Divide scallops between two plates; pour sauce over them. Garnish as desired.

Makes 2 appetizer servings.

Note: To make Garlic Butter, in mixer add 1 chopped shallot, 2 cloves chopped garlic, 2 tablespoons chopped fresh parsley and a little salt and pepper to ½ cup softened butter.

Mix, form into a log and cut off pats as needed. Or wrap with foil and freeze.

To make Basil Butter, substitute 2 tablespoons chopped fresh basil for garlic cloves and 1 tablespoon of the parsley.

Salade Panachee a l'Huile d'Olive (Mixed Green Salad With Olive Oil Vinaigrette)

¾ head Romaine lettuce
¾ head red leaf lettuce
1 head Belgian endive
4 large fresh mushrooms, sliced
4 ounces sliced hearts of palm
1 carrot, cut in thin slivers
1 Golden Delicious apple, peeled, cored and sliced
Olive Oil Vinaigrette
1 medium tomato, cut in wedges

Wash greens, pat dry, tear in bite-size pieces and chill. To serve: combine greens with mushrooms, hearts of palm slices, carrot and apple slices. Toss lightly with dressing and garnish with tomato wedges.

Serves 6.

Olive Oil Vinaigrette
½ cup red wine vinegar
1½ cups extra virgin olive oil
1 teaspoon Dijon mustard
1 teaspoon fresh chopped shallots
Salt and pepper

Whisk vinegar with olive oil. Stir in mustard, shallots and salt and pepper to taste.

Soupe de Legumes aux Fruits de Mer (Clear Vegetable Soup With Seafood)

½ cup baby carrots, diced (or leave whole if small)
½ cup thin fresh green beans, cut in 1-inch pieces
½ cup diced leeks
½ cup diced celery
½ cup diced turnips
1 cup peeled, diced potatoes
2 tablespoons unsalted butter
1 quart vegetable stock
2 ounces lump crabmeat
4 ounces baby shrimp
4 ounces sea or bay scallops
1 lobster tail
1 cup peeled, diced potatoes
4 tablespoons chopped cilantro (fresh coriander or Chinese parsley)
Salt and pepper

Prepare all vegetables; reserve potatoes. Melt butter in large casserole and saute all vegetables except potatoes 1 to 2 minutes.

Add the vegetable stock and simmer 10 to 15 minutes.

Add seafood, potato and chopped cilantro and simmer 2 to 3 minutes, just until seafood is barely done. Season to taste with salt and pepper.

To serve: Ladle into bowls dividing seafood equally. Garnish with cilantro if desired.

Serves 4.

Note: Chef Dominique Dahmani does not recommend substituting chicken broth for vegetable stock because it changes the taste of the soup. You can make your own stock by simmering some chopped celery, carrots and onion with water and seasonings for about 30 minutes.

At La Tour d'Argent, the vegetables are "turned" or sculpted into small pieces. If you have the time, this produces a more attractive soup than dicing the vegetables.

Noisettes d'Agneau au Basilic (Lamb Medallions With Basil Sauce)

1 pound lamb loin or fillet, cleaned, trimmed and cut into medallions
Salt and pepper
2 tablespoons clarified butter
1 shallot, chopped
¾ cup dry white wine
1 cup demi-glaze (can use jarred commercial product)
2 tablespoons heavy (whipping) cream
1 tablespoon chopped basil
2 ounces Basil Butter (see recipe)

Salt and pepper the lamb medallions. Saute in clarified butter until brown, 2 to 3 minutes on each side.

Remove lamb from pan and drain excess fat. Add the shallot, white wine, demi-glaze, cream and chopped basil. Cook 3 or 4 minutes to reduce.

Just before serving, add Basil Butter. Divide lamb medallions between 2 plates and pour sauce over them.

Serve with steamed vegetables such as snow peas, baby carrots and tiny potatoes.

Serves 2.

Champignons Sautes au Beurre d'Ail (Mushrooms Sauteed With Garlic Butter)

2 tablespoons unsalted butter
1 teaspoon chopped shallots
10 large fresh mushrooms, sliced
1 teaspoon chopped garlic
1 tablespoon chopped fresh parsley
   Salt and pepper to taste

Melt butter in saute pan. Add chopped shallots and cook 1 minute so they will lose their acidity.

Add mushrooms, garlic, parsley and salt and pepper to taste and saute until mushrooms are done.

Serves 2.

Hot Apple Tart With Cream and Apricot Sauce

1 recipe Puff Pastry (use favorite recipe, purchase from baker or buy frozen)
   Pastry Cream
4 Golden Delicious apples, peeled, cored and sliced very thin
   Sugar
   Apricot Sauce
   Whipped cream (optional for garnish)

Prepare puff pastry (use favorite recipe calling for about 2 cups flour and 8 ounces butter, or purchase). Keep cold.

Refrigerate remainder while working with one portion. Roll puff pastry out ¼-inch thick and about 6 inches wide.*

Spread Pastry Cream on top. Arrange sliced apples over top and sprinkle with sugar. Place on baking sheet and bake in 450-degree oven 15 minutes. Remove from oven, cut into squares, rectangles or desired shapes. Pour warm Apricot Sauce over it. Serve warm with whipping cream, if desired.

Serves 4 to 6.

*At la Tour d'Argent the tarts are made in 6-inch rounds and are garnished with cream and fresh berries.

Pastry Cream
3 egg yolks
1 cup sugar
½ cup (about 2 ounces) all-purpose flour
3 cups scalded milk (heat until bubbles form at edges, just to boiling)
   Dash of vanilla

Combine egg yolks, sugar and flour with wire whip or in electric mixer. Add hot milk while mixing, transfer to a saucepan and cook over medium heat until thickened, stirring almost constantly. Remove from heat; stir in vanilla. Set aside.

Apricot Sauce
10 ripe apricots, peeled, pitted and mashed
½ cup sugar

Mash apricots or blend in blender with sugar. Transfer to saucepan and cook over medium until thick, about 10 minutes. (Can cook, then puree in blender.) Keep warm. Serve as sauce with hot apple tart.

La Tour d'Argent
2011 Ella Blvd. & T.C. Jester
Houston 77008
864-9864

Magnolia Bar & Grill

FAVORITES

Crawfish Bisque
Crawfish Etouffee
Magnolia Salad
Seafood-Stuffed Eggplant
Baked Duck With Rice Dressing
White Chocolate Mousse

Texans, especially those along the Gulf Coast, have long had an appetite for Cajun food, but three young "missionaries" from southwestern Louisiana have given Houstonians a special appreciation of the spirited Cajun flavors and lifestyle.

In 1983, Floyd Landry (of the famous Louisiana restaurant family) and cousins Jim Gossen and Jody Larriviere, friends since childhood in Lafayette, Louisiana, transformed a restaurant on Richmond and Fountain View in Southwest Houston into a Cajun outpost.

"We dedicated ourselves to the preservation of good South Louisiana cooking," says Larriviere. That means tangy oysters on the half shell (shucked only to order), cornmeal-fried catfish, spicy chicken wings, gumbo, frog legs, stuffed flounder and oyster, shrimp and beef poorboys.

The friends grew up hunting and fishing and they have gifted ways with nature's bounty, especially duck (baked and served with their superb rice dressing, it's a revelation) and with crawfish and softshell crabs.

Magnolia Bar & Grill is a fun place to go for a drink, for Sunday brunch, to whoop it up at Mardi Gras or to take visitors to introduce them to Cajun food.

Star Attractions

★ Architectural design and interior by Kirksey-Meyers. An impressive antique mahogany bar with massive onyx rail. Potted trees filled with twinkle lights. Plantation shutters, lazy ceiling fans and fresh greenery give that genteel southern Louisiana feeling.

★ Two TVs keep bar customers up to date on the game of the season.

★ Changing displays of photographs, graphics and paintings of Louisiana scenes. Black-and-white photo enlargements in the main dining room are by Elmore Morgan Sr., whose work is familiar in National Geographic Magazine.

★ Seasonal specialties—crawfish (the softshell crawfish are truly unique), pee wee softshell crab appetizers and oysters.

★ Charcoal grilled steaks.

★ Home-style Cajun cooking and family specialties such as Potatoes Landry.

★ Accommodation for small private parties (Magnolia's Mardi Gras party is always pleasant to excess in the true Cajun tradition.)

★ Casual dress. Reservations not required.

★ Deck with umbrella tables.

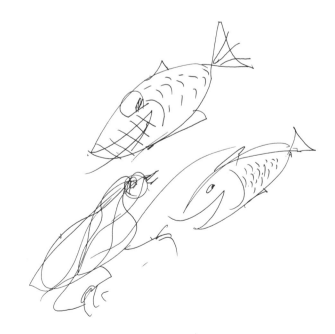

Crawfish Bisque with Stuffed Shells

½ cup vegetable oil
1 cup flour
2 cups chopped yellow onion
½ cup chopped celery
½ cup canned whole tomatoes
    Salt and cayenne to taste
1 gallon boiling water
    Stuffed Crawfish Shells
1 pound crawfish tail meat

Make a roux: Heat oil in large pot (preferably black iron) and stir in flour. Stir constantly while cooking over low heat until it is a dark reddish-brown, about 30 to 45 minutes.

Add onion, celery and tomatoes and saute 5 minutes. Add seasoning and boiling water. Simmer slowly 2 hours.

Meanwhile, make stuffed crawfish shells for garnish. Makes about 1 gallon.

Crawfish Shell Stuffing
½ cup chopped yellow onion, sauteed in butter
    Cooked crawfish tails (½ cup chopped for stuffing and 1 pound cooked for bisque)
½ cup seasoned breadcrumbs
2 tablespoons chopped fresh parsley
2 tablespoons chopped green onion
16 cleaned crawfish shells, boiled

Combine onion, ½ cup chopped crawfish tails, breadcrumbs, parsley and green onion and fill crawfish shells.

Add remaining stuffing to bisque.

To serve: Add crawfish tails to bisque and garnish with stuffed shells.

Serves 8.

Crawfish Etouffee

1 pound cleaned crawfish tails (can buy commercially)
1 teaspoon salt
¼ teaspoon cayenne pepper
1 stick margarine or butter
1 medium onion, finely chopped
1 heaping teaspoon all-purpose flour
    Crawfish fat and water to make ¾ cup
2 very thin slices lemon
1 heaping tablespoon tomato paste
1 garlic clove, minced
1 tablespoon chopped fresh parsley
1 tablespoon green onion
    Hot steamed rice

Use a saucepan with a tight-fitting lid (etouffee is the French word for smothered). Season crawfish tails with salt and pepper; set aside.

Melt butter, add onion and cook over medium heat until tender. Stir in the flour; blend well.

Add water, crawfish fat, lemon, tomato paste and garlic. Cook slowly, about 20 minutes, adding a little water occasionally.

When sauce is done, add crawfish tails and cover pan. Cook 8 minutes. Season again to taste. Add parsley and green onion; cook 2 minutes longer.

Serve over steamed rice. Garlic bread and green salad also are good accompaniments.

Serves 4 to 6.

Magnolia Salad Dressing/Seafood Salad

5 hard-cooked eggs, diced
1 green and 1 red bell pepper, diced
4 ounces black olives, sliced
1 ounce anchovies, chopped
8 ounces Creole mustard
12 ounces red wine vinegar
4 ounces Louanna cottonseed oil
Cooked, peeled shrimp and crawfish or lump crab (use a total of 3 ounces seafood per salad)

Mix diced eggs, bell pepper, olives and anchovies with Creole mustard.

Stir in wine vinegar. Slowly add oil, whisking until thoroughly mixed. Lightly toss with salad greens of choice.

Serves 4.

For seafood salad: Add 3 ounces shrimp, crawfish and/or crab for each salad. To serve: Toss shrimp and/or crawfish lightly with greens and dressing; arrange crabmeat on top of greens.

Note: Dressing may be made in food processor by combining anchovies, mustard and vinegar, adding oil in a slow steady stream, then folding in finely diced eggs, pepper and olives by hand.

Seafood Stuffed Eggplant

6 medium eggplants
2 medium mirlitons (chayote squash)
¼ pound margarine
½ large onion
2 cloves garlic, pressed
1 rib celery, chopped
½ bunch green onions, cut in 1-inch pieces
1 pound small shrimp, cleaned and peeled
1 pound crabmeat
Salt and pepper to taste
1 cup seasoned dry breadcrumbs

Parboil eggplant in a small amount of water until skin is soft. Remove from water, cut in half lengthwise, scoop out pulp and reserve.

Peel mirlitons, slice in eighths and parboil in a small amount of water until soft, but not mushy. Drain.

In skillet, melt margarine and cook eggplant pulp, onion, garlic, celery, mirlitons, green onion and shrimp until tender, about 5 minutes.

Add crab, salt and pepper to taste. Use 1 cup breadcrumbs or enough to stiffen mixture to bind.

Refill eggplant shells with mixture and bake in 350-degree oven 10 to 15 minutes. Top with more breadcrumbs, and serve.

Serves 6.

Baked Duck with Rice Dressing

1   clove garlic
     Salt
½   teaspoon black pepper
     Cayenne pepper
1   (5-pound) duck
     Paprika

Puree garlic with ½ teaspoon salt, black pepper and ½ teaspoon cayenne. Sprinkle duck cavity with mixture. Rub skin with paprika, salt and cayenne. Place duck, breast side up, in roasting pan. Bake at 275 degrees 5½ hours or until done. Baste every 30 minutes with drippings and sprinkle lightly with paprika after each basting. Serve with Rice Dressing (Dirty Rice).

Serves 2.

Rice Dressing
1   teaspoon salt
1   teaspoon cayenne pepper
½   teaspoon black pepper
1   onion, diced
½   green bell pepper, diced
1   rib celery, diced
2   tablespoons oil
½   pound chicken gizzards
½   pound chicken livers
1   pound ground beef, crumbled
1   pound ground pork, crumbled
1   bunch green onions, chopped
1   bunch parsley, chopped
     Hot cooked rice

Combine salt, cayenne, pepper, onion, bell pepper and celery and saute in oil in pot until tender. Remove from pot.

Saute chicken gizzards in skillet, adding about 2 inches of water. Boil until liquid has evaporated and gizzards have begun to fry again. Repeat 2 or 3 times until gizzards are cooked. Add cut-up livers, ground beef and pork and saute them, adding more water and simmering until liquid is reduced to a gravy consistency.

Add cooked vegetables and cook long enough for flavors to blend. Stir in chopped green onion and parsley. Mix one part of dressing mixture to 1½ parts of hot cooked rice.

Serves 12 or more.

White Chocolate Mousse

½   pound white chocolate
⅛   pound (½ stick) unsalted butter
2   cups heavy (whipping) cream
8   egg whites, at room temperature
⅛   pound (2 ounces) powdered sugar
     Whipped cream and mint leaves for garnish (optional)

Melt chocolate and butter in a metal bowl over a pan of boiling water, stirring occasionally to blend. (Or melt in microwave on low power; stir to smooth.) Cool to room temperature.

Whip cream (chill cream, bowl and beaters thoroughly) until stiff. Whip egg whites in electric mixer bowl until stiff, blending in powdered sugar.

In large bowl, combine melted chocolate, cream and egg whites. Fold together gently with a plastic spatula. When blended, pipe the mousse into champagne or wine glasses using a pastry bag with a star tip. Refrigerate mousse until set. Serve with a dollop of whipped cream and a fresh mint leaf for garnish.

Serves 6 to 8.

Mousse also can be served from a large souffle or dessert dish, but should be thoroughly chilled before serving.

Magnolia Bar & Grill
6000 Richmond Ave.
Houston, 77057
781-6207

Montesano Ristorante Italiano

Montesano is a marriage of Italian home cooking and fine wines, and the mood and the food change with the seasons. You would never guess that the stylish restaurant, with its splashing fountains, round bar, arched niches and vaulted ceilings, used to be a down-home Texas steak house.

Owner Antonio Mingalone, who grew up in the restaurant business and is a former restaurant manager for the Waldorf-Astoria in New York, has transformed the rustic building into an Italian family restaurant. His parents, who retired several years ago, came from southern Italy for a visit and have stayed on to help. His father Vito is at the door to welcome guests in Italian and his mother Anna (her maiden name was Montesano) presides over the kitchen. She is there early and late, says Mingalone, and she even grows the herbs for the restaurant.

There is almost a theatrical quality to the decor. If it's spring, silky pastel ribbons may swirl like Maypole streamers from the classic columns in the dining room. If it's fall, rust, browns and leaf colors predominate. Restful Italian music flows through the air as counterpoint to the splashing water from a massive fountain, which Mingalone's uncle had hand-carved in Italy as a gift. Mauve upholstery, pink linens, green plants, fresh flowers and paintings (a gift from another uncle) add to the relaxing atmosphere.

An antique table greets guests to the dining room with an incredible array of mouth-watering antipasto dishes such as roasted peppers, aged Italian ham with figs and carpaccio, paper-thin strips of raw beef dressed with garlic, peppers and olive oil.

The wine list, which took more than a year to develop, reflects Mingalone's love of fine wines. No wine goes on the list unless he has tasted it, and sometimes the dishes that go on the menu are chosen to compliment the wines instead of the other way around. He also buys and stores wines for some of his best customers.

Mingalone is from a small seaport town, Taranto, but the menu reflects various regional soups, pasta and veal dishes. "My menu is made up of things I like, done my way. They are not traditionally Italian and not traditionally American."

Star Attractions

★ Down-to-earth Italian cooking done with care.

★ Beautiful seasonal menu covers with paintings by Ken Boehnert; you'll want to frame them.

★ Small private dining rooms. Wine cellar for private parties.

★ Fixed-price fast lunch—soup, salad, entree, dessert and beverage—for the businessperson in a hurry.

★ Antipasto table with wide selection of appetizers.

★ Seasonal specialties such as porcini mushrooms.

★ Regional specialties such as perciatelli, a tubular pasta with a spicy fresh tomato-basil sauce; Delicatezza Della Spangna, red Spanish shrimp sauteed in wine; Eggplant a la Mama, one of Montesano's most popular dishes, and Coniglio Don Vito, roasted rabbit marinated with fresh herbs (it's named for Mingalone's father because it's his favorite dish).

★ Excellent wine list including fine vintages from Antinori, Mastroberardino, Gaja and other top Italian winemakers.

★ Exceptional pastry cart and dessert list— Zuppa Inglese, Cannoli, Spumoni (made by Mingalone's wife), Chocolate Bombe and tiramisu ("tier-ah-MEE-sue," the Italian mascarpone cheese and ladyfinger dessert).

Eggplant Della Mamma

2	medium eggplants
½	cup olive oil
½	pound sweet Italian sausage, diced
3	cloves garlic, minced
½	cup white wine
6	fresh basil leaves, chopped
1	cup breadcrumbs
	Crushed hot red pepper flakes
3	tablespoons chopped fresh parsley
	Salt and pepper to taste
1½	cups grated Fontina or Mozzarella cheese

Cut eggplants in half lengthwise and scoop out insides leaving a ½-inch shell.

Dice eggplant pulp and saute in hot oil 2 minutes over medium heat.

Add diced sausage and saute until cooked, about 4 or 5 minutes.

Add garlic, wine, basil, breadcrumbs, crushed red pepper flakes and parsley. Blend well and add salt and pepper to taste. Stir in cheese.

Stuff mixture in eggplant shells and place on baking sheet or in baking dish.

Bake at 350 degrees 30 minutes, or until golden brown.

Serves 4.

Delicatezza Della Spangna (Red Spanish Shrimp Sauteed in Wine)

2   pounds giant red Spanish shrimp (do not substitute any other shrimp—see note)
¼   pound butter
4   cloves garlic, chopped
1   tablespoon chopped fresh basil
½   cup white wine
1   tablespoon chopped fresh parsley
    Juice of 1 lemon
    Salt and pepper to taste

Leave shrimp in their shells but slice the underside to butterfly them.

Melt half the butter in a skillet large enough to hold all the shrimp. Saute on one side 2 minutes over medium heat. Turn once; saute until done, about 2 minutes more. Quickly add garlic, basil, wine and parsley. Add lemon juice.

Bring to a boil and add remaining butter, beating or whisking until sauce thickens. Season with salt and pepper and serve immediately.

Serves 4.

Note: This recipe was developed at Montesano's with the large red Spanish shrimp which are sometimes available at specialty fish markets. Mingalone says other types of shrimp do not produce the same distinctive results.

Crostini di Fontina
(Fried Sandwich Appetizer)

½ eggplant, peeled and sliced
    Flour for dredging
6   eggs, beaten
6   tablespoons olive oil
8   ounces Fontina cheese
2   slices prosciutto (thin Italian ham)
4   anchovy fillets
8   slices white bread

Dip eggplant slices in flour and beaten egg and saute in hot oil 1 minute on each side until golden brown. Drain on paper towels.

Layer eggplant, grated cheese, prosciutto and anchovies on 4 bread slices. Top with remaining bread slices. Gently dip in beaten egg to coat, turning the sandwiches once.

Heat oil in non-stick skillet large enough to hold sandwiches. Saute until brown on one side.

Carefully turn with spatula and brown on the other side until cheese is melted in the middle.

Cut each into 4 wedges and serve on a bed of marinara sauce (use your favorite recipe or buy bottled.)

Cotoletta Milanese
(Veal Cutlet Milanese)

1   pound veal cutlets, pounded thin
    Flour for dredging
4   eggs, beaten
½   cup freshly grated Parmesan cheese
1   cup breadcrumbs
3   tablespoons olive oil
3   cloves garlic, minced
6   basil leaves, chopped
½   cup julienned prosciutto
1   cup diced plum tomatoes
1   cup chicken stock
    Salt and pepper to taste

Lightly dredge cutlets in flour. Dip in a batter of combined eggs and Parmesan, then in breadcrumbs.

Heat oil in saute pan and saute cutlets until done, about 2 minutes on each side. Remove from pan.

Add garlic, basil, prosciutto, tomatoes and stock to pan. Cook 1 minute. Add salt and pepper to taste.

Pour sauce over cutlets and serve.

Serves 3 or 4.

Perciatelli al Fuoco di Roma
(Perciatelli Pasta Roma)

1	pound perciatelli pasta (long tubular pasta)
1	onion, diced
1	tablespoon extra virgin olive oil
4	cloves garlic, minced
½	cup white wine
4	cups seeded chopped plum tomatoes
1	teaspoon crushed hot red pepper flakes
¼	cup julienned prosciutto
2	ounces dried Italian porcini mushrooms (soak in ½ cup chicken stock) or 6 ounces fresh porcini mushrooms
½	cup grated Romano cheese

Cook pasta al dente (firm to the tooth) while making sauce.

Saute onion in oil 3 minutes. Add garlic and saute 30 seconds, then add wine, tomatoes, pepper flakes, prosciutto, mushrooms and broth they soaked in. Simmer over low heat 30 minutes.

Toss with well-drained pasta and dust with cheese.

Serves 4.

Tiramisu

Tiramisu (pronounced "tier-ah-MEE-sue") is a popular Italian dessert. There are many versions but all include similar combinations of mascarpone cheese, eggs, Italian ladyfingers (savoiardi), espresso and chocolate.

3   eggs, separated, or 3 egg yolks (see Notes)
3   tablespoons sugar
1   pound mascarpone cheese, softened* Coffee liqueur such as Kahlua
3   tablespoons brandy or rum
1   (7-ounce) package Italian ladyfingers (savoiardi - see Notes)
¾   cup espresso, cooled Dark bittersweet chocolate shavings

Whisk egg yolks with sugar until light. Beat in softened cheese until smooth. Blend in liqueur, then brandy, whisking constantly. (Add liqueur first to prevent brandy curdling the eggs.) If using egg whites, beat until stiff and carefully fold in.

Pour espresso (and if desired 2 more tablespoons Kahlua) into flat shallow pan. Quickly dip 12 ladyfingers, one by one, into mixture; do not over-saturate or tiramisu will be watery. Arrange in 9-inch pie plate or quiche pan.

Spread half the mascarpone mixture over ladyfingers. Sprinkle with chocolate shavings. Dip 12 more ladyfingers into espresso and repeat layers.

Cover tightly with plastic wrap or foil and refrigerate at least 1 hour, preferably overnight.

To serve: Cut in slices or wedges. Garnish with whipped cream and more chocolate shavings, if desired. For individual servings, pile 3 ladyfingers in a pyramid on a dessert plate and pour mascarpone mixture over them. Cover with plastic wrap and chill at least 30 minutes, preferably longer. Garnish with shaved chocolate.

*Mascarpone is an Italian double cream cheese of 60 percent butterfat. It is a fresh (unripened) cheese that originated in Lombardy, Italy, and it has a buttery, pleasantly sourish tang. It resembles a combination of cream cheese and sour cream (which can be used as a substitute).

Use the plain mascarpone for tiramisu; it is sometimes layered with other cheeses such as Gorgonzola, pine nuts or smoked salmon in mascarpone torta.

Because it is so rich, a little goes a long way.

Notes: Italian ladyfingers are drier and larger than American. They are available at Italian specialty markets, some supermarkets (check the bakery, freezer or cookie departments). Some bakeries also make them.

If American ladyfingers are substituted, you will need more. Use the unfilled variety and toast them in a 375-degree oven about 10 minutes to dry them out. Strips of genoise cake also may be substituted.

If desired, beat egg whites until stiff, but not dry, and fold into mascarpone mixture.

Other coffee-flavored liqueurs may be used and chocolate shavings can be bittersweet, sweet or semisweet.

Montesano Ristorante Italiano
6009 Beverly Hill Lane
Houston, 77057
977-4565

Nash D'Amico's Pasta & Clam Bar

However, in only four years, D'Amico also has made a reputation for more upscale dishes such as outstanding ravioli (particularly the salmon ravioli), calamari, veal and Parmesan dishes.

They do four Parmesans—veal, chicken, eggplant and shrimp—and three basic red sauces—sugo (D'Amico's version is a prized family recipe), marinara (used with seafood) and a spicy stew sauce used in the seafood stew and linguine with spicy seafood sauce.

The pasta is made fresh several times a day. Specialties include Fettucine Alfredo, tortellini, straw and hay (paglia y fieno) and linguine.

FAVORITES

Fried Squid (calamari)
Steamed Mussels
New England Clam Chowder
Spinach Pasta
Marinara Sauce
Chicken Parmesan
House Salad

Star Attractions

★ Casual, fun atmosphere. "Tropical" art deco interiors by designer Susan White are an appealing mix of peach, lavender, rose, gray and black.

★ At the Village location, abstract art work of laminated, fired glass by Steve Hecht. The Westheimer location features abstract three-dimensional art by Robert Terrell.

★ Moderate prices: half-price Lite Orders.

★ Bar with full menu for counter service.

★ Specialties such as Chicken Cuscinetti and Chicken Piccata.

★ Home delivery service.

Nash D'Amico's Pasta & Clam Bar is known for home-style Italian cooking and a casual, fun atmosphere with "tropical" Art Deco decor.

The small, informal restaurants (there are now two) flash with neon and chrome and are a gathering spot for young urban professionals. The Village location attracts the crowd from the Texas Medical Center, Rice University Village and Greenway Plaza. The newer Westheimer restaurant draws from the Galleria and Southwest area.

Owner Nash D'Amico and executive chef Gary Malloy have worked out the simple menu which leans to southern Italian food. It includes classic favorites such as spaghetti with meatballs, lasagna, fettucine, mussels, clams, cannoli and cheesecake.

Fried Squid

1   pound squid
1   cup all-purpose flour
2   quarts oil for deep frying
1   teaspoon salt
½   teaspoon white pepper

Wash squid under cold running water and remove skin. Turn the back side up and cut through, removing the backbone and exposing the insides.

Remove the ink sac by pinching the tentacles apart from the sac. Squeeze excess fluid out and discard the mouth. Wash inside with cold water.

Slice squid into ¼-inch rings. Dust with flour.

Fry in deep, hot (375-degree) oil, about 2½ minutes, until they float. Drain on paper towels and sprinkle with salt and pepper.

Serves 2.

Steamed Mussels

2   pounds mussels (about 40) in shells
¼   cup oil
½   cup white wine

Clean mussels in several changes of cold water, scrub shells and remove beards (black hairs from middle).

Heat oil and wine in skillet and add mussels. Cover tightly and steam over medium-high heat about 8 to 10 minutes, until shells open.

Serve with natural broth or strain off and add desired sauce.

Serves 2 to 4 as appetizers or main dish.

Note: Mussels should be purchased live in the shells and shells should be tightly closed. They are very perishable and should be used as soon as possible. Store in the refrigerator no longer than two days.

New England Clam Chowder

    Roux (1 cup melted butter, ⅔ cup flour)
¾   cup finely chopped bacon
⅔   cup finely chopped onion
1   clove garlic, finely chopped
4   cups diced, peeled potatoes, boiled
1½   cups fresh minced clams
3   cups heavy (whipping) cream
1   quart clam juice

Make roux of 1 cup melted butter and ⅔ cup flour.

Saute bacon, strain off the fat. Add onion and garlic and cook another 10 minutes. Drain potatoes and set aside.

Boil clams in water to cover just until done. Strain and set aside. In large dutch oven or pot, combine bacon, onions, diced potatoes, clams, cream and clam juice. Bring to a boil.

Stir in thickened roux, add salt and pepper to taste and heat through, stirring.

Makes 1½ gallons.

Nash D'Amico's House Salad

1   head Romaine lettuce
1   tomato, cut in wedges
1   cucumber, thinly sliced

Wash lettuce and tear in bite-size pieces. Slice tomato and cucumber. Toss lightly with just enough mayonnaise dressing to coat lightly.

Makes 3 salads.

Mayonnaise Dressing
1   carrot, washed, pared and cut in 1-inch pieces
1½ tablespoons capers
1   rib celery, cut in pieces
1   small clove garlic, cut in half
1½ green onions, cut in pieces
1½ tablespoons Worcestershire sauce
    Juice of 1 lemon
1   quart mayonnaise
    Salt and pepper

Combine carrot, capers, celery, garlic and green onion and process in food processor until finely ground.

Add Worcestershire and lemon juice and combine with mayonnaise. Add salt and pepper to taste. Makes about 5 cups. Refrigerate to store.

Chicken Parmesan

1   pound boneless, skinless chicken breast, cut in half
1   cup flour
2   eggs, beaten
    Seasoned bread crumbs
2   tablespoons oil
    Red wine
    Freshly grated Parmesan or Romano cheese
1   cup suga (red spaghetti sauce) or marinara sauce
1   cup grated Mozzarella cheese
    Chopped fresh parsley for garnish

Pound chicken breast with a mallet until about ⅛-inch thick. Place flour, beaten eggs and bread crumbs in separate shallow dishes.

Dust chicken with flour. Dip in beaten egg, then in bread crumbs.

Heat oil in ovenproof skillet and saute chicken on both sides until golden brown. Pour off excess oil.

Add a splash of red wine to skillet and heat a minute or so. Top each chicken breast with about ½ cup suga or marinara sauce and a generous sprinkling of Parmesan.

Cover with ½ cup grated Mozzarella and run skillet under broiler until cheese is melted. Sprinkle with chopped parsley and serve with spaghetti or fettucine with marinara sauce on the side.

Serves 2.

Spinach Pasta

½   pound fresh spinach
2   cups all-purpose flour
2   eggs

Wash spinach in several changes of fresh water. Place in saucepan with only the water that clings to the leaves and cook, covered, about 8 minutes. Cool, squeeze dry and finely chop.

Shape flour into a mound, make a well in the center and add spinach and beaten eggs. Incorporate flour gradually into mixture and stir to a paste. Continue incorporating flour and stirring until mixture forms a ball.

Knead on a flat surface about 7 minutes, until dough is smooth and satiny. Cover (with towel or bowl) and let rest 15 minutes.

Place dough on a lightly floured surface (use as little flour as possible). Roll out ⅛-inch thick. Put through pasta machine or cut by hand into strands or other desired shape.

To cut by hand, roll up sheet of pasta tightly like a jelly roll from the long side. Slice in thickness desired, unroll each strand and arrange on a lightly floured surface or towel to dry for a few minutes. Work quickly and don't let pasta dry out too much. Makes about 1 pound.

To cook: Bring a large pot of salted water to a rolling boil (use 4 quarts water to 1 pound pasta). Add 1 tablespoon oil. Drop pasta into water, let water return to the boil and boil until pasta is al dente (firm to the tooth), about 3 to 4 minutes for fresh pasta. Test by removing a strand.

Drain pasta in a colander and return it to the pot. Toss lightly with 1 or 2 tablespoons melted butter. Serve immediately.

Serves 2 to 4.

Marinara Sauce

¼   cup olive oil
4   tablespoons chopped garlic
5   tablespoons chopped fresh basil
3   tablespoons chopped fresh parsley
4   tomatoes (2 pounds), peeled and pureed, or 32 ounces canned peeled tomatoes
    Salt and pepper to taste

Heat olive oil in pot over medium heat until clear. Add garlic, basil and parsley and simmer slowly for a few minutes.

Add pureed tomatoes and simmer 1 hour.

Skim foam off top and add salt and pepper to taste while cooking. Makes 3 cups. Use as a sauce with seafood or pasta.

Nash D'Amico's Pasta & Clam Bar
2421 Times Blvd. in the Village, 521-3010
Houston, 77005
5640 Westheimer, 960-1230
Houston, 77027

Ninfa's

Ninfa's is one of the business success stories of the past two decades in Houston. Its humble beginning was a 10-table taqueria which Ninfa Laurenzo opened next to her home near the Ship Channel in 1973.

A recent widow, her "assets" at the time were five children and $16 cash. The family pulled together and on the first day of business they sold 256 tacos. Today the family owns ten restaurants (nine in Houston and one in Dallas) that ring up sales of more than $20 million a year.

The menus are based on Mexican home cooking, the kind of food Ninfa Laurenzo grew up with or discovered during extensive travels. The restaurants are known for authentic regional Mexican food (not Tex-Mex) and for their colorful decor, "Gracias" slogan and brightly colored parrot logo, which symbolizes love.

If there were a Mexican culinary hall of fame in Houston it would include at least three Ninfa's signature dishes—the singular green sauce; tacos al carbon, which are now trademarked Tacos a la Ninfa, and Ninfaritas, a potent version of the Margarita.

Tacos al Carbon are similar to fajitas, but the meat is cut in chunks and rolled in flour tortillas in the kitchen before serving. For fajitas, the meat is sliced and served on sizzling platters and guests assemble their own.

Ninfa's sauces are still made fresh two or three times a day, flour tortillas are made by hand and everything is cooked fresh daily.

Star Attractions

★ Nine convenient locations in Houston: 2704 Navigation, 6154 Westheimer, 9333-B Katy Freeway (Echo Lane), 8507 Gulf Freeway, 231 Bammel Rd. (FM 1960), 600 Travis, 3601 Kirby Dr. at Richmond, 9725 Bissonnet and 14737 Memorial.

★ Festive party atmosphere—bright colors, small fountain patios in some restaurants, rustic tables and chairs, colorful banners. Popular place to celebrate birthdays and other special occasions.

★ Authentic regional home-style Mexican cooking. Specialties include Queso a la Parrilla, a melted white cheese, mushroom, onion and pepper dish as it's done in Parrilla; flautas; carnitas, bits of boneless roast pork served with green and red sauces; guacamole and flour tortillas.

★ Some light dishes are available or small or half portions of selected dishes may be ordered.

★ Extensive list of off-the-menu specials.

★ Happy Hour with free buffet at three locations—Gulf Freeway, Kirby at Richmond and Westheimer.

★ Full catering service.

★ Complimentary red and green sauce with chips and tortillas.

★ Diners can watch women making the flour tortillas by hand on comals (griddles) in the dining rooms.

★ Mexican soda waters in fruit flavors. Special after-dinner coffee drinks.

Fajitas with Marinated Onions

2   skirt steaks, no more than ¾ inch thick
1   large orange
2   lemons
¼   cup each pineapple juice, white wine, water and soy sauce
1   clove garlic, minced
1   tablespoon black pepper
3   dried arbol chilies
3   tablespoons clarified butter
16   to 20 flour tortillas, warmed
    Marinated Onions (recipe follows)
    Tomato slices and green pepper rings for garnish

Grate 1 tablespoon orange peel and 2 teaspoons lemon peel. Squeeze ¼ cup orange juice and ¼ cup lemon juice. Combine peel and juices, wine, water, soy sauce, garlic, pepper, whole chilies and butter in large shallow non-metal dish; stir.

Trim excess fat from skirt steak and peel off any membrane. If meat is thicker than ¾-inch at thickest part, cut in half lengthwise so it will cook quickly. Place skirt steaks in mixture, turn to coat, cover dish with plastic wrap and marinate at room temperature no longer than 2 hours.

Prepare charcoal grill or preheat broiler. Grill fajitas 3 inches above very hot coals (or about 4 inches below broiler) for a short time, about 5 or 6 minutes per side. Cut crosswise into finger-length strips.

Place on hot platter with Marinated Onions. Garnish with tomato slices and green pepper rings if desired.

To assemble fajita, place some beef strips down center of warm flour tortillas with Marinated Onions. Add desired condiments such as Refried Beans, Guacamole, Pico de Gallo and sour cream.

Makes 8 to 10 servings.

Marinated Onions
1   cup water
½   cup soy sauce
1   tablespoon beef base or 4 beef bouillon cubes, dissolved
2   dried arbol chilies or 2 fresh jalapenos, stems removed and chopped
2   large onions, sliced in rings (2 cups)

Combine water, soy sauce, beef base and chilies (remove stems and crush) or jalapenos.

Separate onions into rings and add to marinade covering onions completely.

Cover with plastic wrap and marinate in refrigerator several hours or overnight.

To heat: Lift onions from marinade with slotted spoon and heat in top part of a double boiler over simmering water. Serve with fajitas.

Makes 6 to 8 servings.

Pork Fajitas: Use boneless pork tenderloin cut ½-inch thick.

Chicken Fajitas: Use 2 to 2¼ pounds boneless, skinless chicken breasts, pounded to ¾-inch thick. Marinate in mixture of 3 tablespoons white wine, 6 tablespoons melted butter, 1 tablespoon soy sauce, 2 teaspoons garlic powder and 1 teaspoon black pepper.

Note: Flank steak or round steak may be substituted for skirt steak.

Pico de Gallo

Pico de gallo literally translates to "rooster's beak" in Spanish. It is used as a relish with many Mexican dishes, especially fajitas and is excellent with fish and chicken.

1   medium-size ripe tomato, diced
1   medium onion, diced (½ cup)
3   to 4 fresh jalapenos, stems removed and chopped
    Juice of ½ lime
12   sprigs fresh cilantro, minced

Combine tomato, onion, jalapenos and lime juice. Add cilantro. Makes about 1½ cups. Best when made as needed and used fresh.

Note: For best texture, use a ripe tomato that is still slightly firm and pinkish in color (drain well) and a Texas 1015 or other mild, sweet spring onion.

Refried Beans

1   pound dried pinto beans
8   cups water
1   small garlic clove, mashed
1   slice bacon, cut in ½-inch pieces
1½   teaspoons salt
1½   tablespoons pork lard or bacon fat
1½   teaspoons ground cumin (cominos)
     Shredded Monterey Jack cheese

Wash beans under cold running water, pick over them and discard any stones. Bring water to a boil in large pot (there should be enough to cover beans by two inches). Add beans, garlic, bacon and salt. Return to a boil, reduce heat, cover and simmer 1 to 2½ hours, or until beans are tender.

Drain beans in colander set over large bowl. Measure 1 cup liquid. Reserve and refrigerate any remaining bean liquid for future use.

Place part of beans in food processor, add ¼ cup reserved bean liquid, cover and process just until beans are mashed. Do not puree. Turn into a large bowl and repeat using ¼ cup bean liquid for each batch. Beans should be moist. Set aside.

Melt lard in large, heavy skillet. Add cumin and stir until lard is dissolved, about 2 or 3 minutes. Add beans gradually, stirring constantly to mix well. When all the beans have been added, cook over low heat, stirring constantly, 20 minutes. Do not let beans stick to skillet or burn.

Turn into a heatproof serving dish. Sprinkle with shredded cheese and place under broiler until cheese melts.

Makes 6 cups.

Leftover beans may be reheated with reserved bean liquid, broth or water.

Diet Alert: Use polyunsaturated oil instead of lard or bacon fat and use low-fat or part-skim milk cheese.

Ninfa's Green Sauce

3   medium-size green tomatoes, coarsely chopped
4   tomatillos (Mexican green tomatoes in a papery husk), cleaned and chopped
1   to 2 jalapenos, stemmed and coarsely chopped
3   small garlic cloves
3   medium-size ripe avocados
4   sprigs cilantro
1   teaspoon salt
1½   cups imitation sour cream

Combine chopped tomatoes, tomatillos, jalapenos and garlic in a saucepan. Bring to a boil, reduce heat and simmer 15 minutes or until tomatoes are soft. Remove from heat and let cool slightly.

Peel, pit and slice avocados; set aside. Place tomato mixture with part of the avocados, cilantro and salt in food processor (probably will have to do in batches) and process until smooth.

Turn into a large bowl. Stir in sour cream, cover with plastic wrap and refrigerate.

Makes 4 to 5 cups.

Serve in small bowls as a dip for tortilla chips. Promptly refrigerate leftovers.

Note: Handle jalapenos carefully; hot peppers can irritate skin and eyes.

Mexican Rice

5   to 6 strands saffron*
3   cups chicken broth (preferably homemade), divided
3   tablespoons oil (original recipe calls for ⅓ cup lard)
3   ounces pork butt, cut in ¼-inch cubes (½ cup)
2   cups long grain rice
¼   cup diced tomato
¼   cup chopped green pepper, divided
¼   cup chopped onion
2   tablespoons bottled pizza sauce
¾   teaspoon ground cumin (cominos)
1   teaspoon salt
¼   teaspoon pepper
¼   teaspoon garlic powder
¼   cup leftover green peas (optional)

Dissolve saffron in 1 cup hot chicken broth; set aside. Keep remaining broth warm.

Heat oil in 6-quart pot. Brown pork in oil, about 4 or 5 minutes. Add rice. Cook 10 to 12 minutes, stirring frequently, until golden.

Place tomato, 2 tablespoons green pepper, onion, pizza sauce, cumin, salt, pepper and garlic powder in blender container.

Add the broth containing saffron; cover and blend until smooth. Stir into rice in saucepot. Add remaining broth and green pepper; bring to a boil.

Reduce heat, cover and simmer 10 to 15 minutes. Stir and cook 2 minutes longer, Add peas.

Turn heat off and let stand about 5 minutes.

Makes 8 to 10 servings.

*Saffron is the most expensive spice in the world. There is no substitute for taste, but turmeric is frequently substituted for color.

Ninfa's Pina Teocali

1   cup pineapple juice
1   cup firmly packed brown sugar
1   teaspoon ground cinnamon
½   cup raisins
1   small ripe pineapple
2   pints coconut ice cream or pineapple sherbet*
    Sliced almonds (optional)

Make Pina Sauce: Combine pineapple juice, sugar, cinnamon and raisins in medium saucepan. Bring to a boil. Reduce heat and simmer 5 minutes. Remove from heat; let cool.

With sharp knife, cut off pineapple top and a slice off the bottom. Cut down in a curved motion to remove shell. Cut 8 (½-inch thick) round slices. Core centers. Grill each side of pineapple rings on a grill or hibachi until lightly browned.

Place one ring on each of 8 dessert dishes. Top with a scoop of ice cream and ¼ cup sauce. Sprinkle with almonds.

Serves 8.

*If coconut ice cream is not available, substitute pineapple sherbet and add ¼ cup coconut liqueur to the Pina Sauce.

Ninfa's
963-9333

Oak'n Bucket

For many of Bob Collins' customers, eating at the Oak'n Bucket is as comfortable as eating at home, and many of them might say the food is better. Since it opened 10 years ago in this little shopping enclave just inside the Loop, the Oak'n Bucket has become a neighborhood institution.

It is a favorite rendezvous for breakfast in the Galleria area, and deals, big and little, are regularly made over coffee. Some loyal customers show up every morning. Others come at least three or four times a week—for lunch while shopping, for dinner or Sunday brunch.

They like the routine, the friendly repartee with Collins and the casual surroundings—comfortable chairs and oak tables, a color scheme of hunter green and beige, brass coach lamps, used brick, ceiling fans and the softening touch of ivy and hanging plants.

They also like the familiar southern-style American cooking—chicken and dumplings, liver and onions, salads, steaks, grits, omelets, oatmeal (in the winter months), fried shrimp, broiled fish and desserts such as bread pudding and pecan pie.

The family feeling is unmistakable. Collins used to work for his father when the senior Collins owned Majors Coffee Shop. Now his father works for him; he does all the pastries and is the fine hand behind the pancakes and waffles. Most of the employees have worked there for years.

Star Attractions

★ Casual, informal atmosphere.

★ Moderate prices.

★ Breakfast served from 6 to 9 a.m. Monday through Friday and from 8 to 11 a.m. Saturday.

★ Fresh home-baked pies, biscuits, sweet rolls and breads; pie of the month featured.

★ Homemade picante sauce.

★ Fresh squeezed juices.

★ Generally, the food is not presalted. Many dishes can be prepared without butter or margarine on request. With 24 hours notice, they will provide sugar-free pies made with no-cholesterol pastry.

Hot Cakes

2   cups all-purpose flour
1   tablespoon plus 1 teaspoon baking
    powder
2   tablespoons sugar
    Pinch of salt
1   cup milk
2   to 4 tablespoons oil
2   eggs, slightly beaten
¼   to ½ teaspoon vanilla

Mix in order given, stirring just until dry ingredients are moistened.

Heat griddle (unless griddle sticks badly, do not grease) until water sprinkled on surface bounces.

Pour about ¼ cup batter on hot griddle for each pancake. Turn when bubbles begin to break on the top.

Add chopped pecans to batter if desired. Also makes excellent waffles. Makes 12 to 14 (4-inch) hot cakes.

Notes: If batter seems too thick, add more milk. If too thin, add more flour. To make well-shaped rounds, pour batter as close to griddle surface as possible, not from above griddle. Turn only once; second side takes about half as long to cook as the first.

Freeze if desired and reheat in microwave.

Oak'n Bucket Cheese Soup

¼   to ⅓ cup each chopped celery,
    carrots and onion
¾   ounce butter (1¾ tablespoons)
    Water
1   teaspoon salt
2   teaspoons chicken bouillon granules
¼   teaspoon white pepper
½   cup flour
1   tablespoon cornstarch
¾   cup milk
4   to 8 ounces grated Longhorn-style
    Cheddar cheese

Saute chopped celery, carrots and onion in melted butter in 3-quart saucepan until they are soft.

Add 4 cups water (or half water, half chicken stock or bouillon) salt, bouillon granules and pepper and bring to a boil.

Mix flour and cornstarch and dissolve in 1 cup cool water. Pour into boiling soup mixture.

Reduce heat and stir with wire whisk. Immediately add milk.

Simmer over low heat until soup comes to a boil. Remove from heat and add cheese. Stir with whisk until melted.

Makes 6 to 8 servings.

Diet Alert: Substitute soft tub vegetable margarine for butter and salt-free seasoning for salt. Use low-sodium bouillon, skim milk and low-fat, low-sodium cheese.

Breast of Chicken

- 1 (4 to 5-ounce) boneless, skinless chicken breast
- 3 ounces milk
  Seasoned breadcrumbs
- 1 teaspoon melted margarine

Clean chicken breast and remove center cartilage. Pound to flatten with a meat cleaver.

Dip in milk, then in breadcrumbs. Pat crumbs completely around chicken. Place on sheet pan and refrigerate covered until chilled.

Saute in skillet in melted margarine, or spray pan with non-stick spray. Turn only once. May be garnished with sauteed onion or lemon wedges and served with Bearnaise or hollandaise sauce.

Prepared chicken breasts freeze well and cook equally well from the frozen state.

Makes 1 to 2 servings.

Fried Mushrooms

- ½ pound medium-size mushrooms
- 1 cup all-purpose flour
- ⅛ teaspoon cayenne pepper
- 1 cup milk
- 1 egg
- 8 ounces crushed saltine crackers
  Oil for deep frying
  Horseradish Dipping Sauce

Wash mushrooms gently or wipe with damp cloth. Remove stems.

Mix flour and cayenne in a shallow pan. Mix milk and egg in a second shallow pan.

Dip mushrooms in milk first, drain and roll in flour. Dip in milk again, drain, then roll in cracker crumbs.

Deep-fry in hot (375-degree) oil and serve hot with Horseradish Dipping Sauce.

Serves 2 to 3.

Horseradish Dipping Sauce
- 1 cup mayonnaise
- 6 ounces prepared horseradish
- ¼ ounce Worcestershire sauce
- ¼ ounce lemon juice
- ¼ ounce prepared mustard

Combine all ingredients and chill. Serve cold as a dipping sauce for fried mushrooms.

French Silk Chocolate Pie

3½ ounces unsweetened baking chocolate
    Sugar
6   ounces (1½ sticks) margarine
    Vanilla
2   eggs
1   (9-inch) baked pieshell, cooled
8   to 10 ounces whipping cream

Melt the chocolate over hot water or in microwave on low power; stir to smooth.

Cream 6 ounces sugar (1 cup less 2 tablespoons) and margarine in mixer until smooth. Blend in cooled chocolate. Add 2 teaspoons vanilla.

Add eggs, one at a time, beating 2 minutes and scraping bowl before adding second egg.

Pour mixture into cooked, cooled pieshell. Cover with plastic wrap to prevent "skin" from forming on surface. Refrigerate at least 3 hours.

Chill cream, bowl and beaters thoroughly. Beat cream until fluffy, adding 2 ounces (3 tablespoons) sugar and 1 teaspoon vanilla.

Gently spread cream over pie. Garnish as desired—with pecans, chopped walnuts or shaved chocolate.

Refrigerate leftovers.

Makes 1 (9-inch) pie.

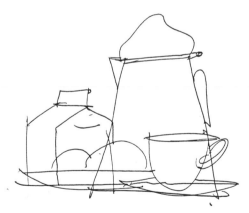

Oak'n Bucket
4204 Westheimer at 2500 Midlane
Houston, 77027
961-7483

Ouisie's

FAVORITES

Grilled Tuna Ouisie With Gremalotta

Shrimp Acapulco

Stuffed Pork Tender

Garlic Mashed Potatoes

*Vegetarian Variation #1 on Lemon
Ginger Rice*

*Roasted Red Bell Peppers With
Bacon and Cheese Sandwich*

Negre en Chemise

Ouisie's is maturing as it leaves adolescence and enters its teen years, but you can continue to expect the unexpected.

Owner Elouise Cooper still rules the range. The chalkboard menu changes daily, and emphasis is on freshness. Ouisie's doesn't even have a commercial freezer.

Classic "World War II" nostalgia food such as pimiento cheese sandwiches and egg salad co-exists on the menu with the newer caviar-topped Ouisie's Spud and innovative fare of the new genre.

Ouisie's specializes in unusual dishes with provocative tastes such as lemon sole topped with shrimp in mint marigold butter or chicken breast stuffed with spinach, Texas goat cheese and pine nuts with linguini or a vegetarian combination featuring stuffed kohlrabi on sauteed watercress.

In addition to Cooper's evolving palate and flair with food, the menu's development also can be attributed to enthusiastic young staff members such as chef David Goldman as well as tasting sessions and adventurous cooking with exotic new ingredients.

Ouisie's is convenient to the Texas Medical Center, Rice University, Museum of Fine Arts, Montrose and Southhampton residential areas and has an upscale Ivy League neighborhood ambiance.

Star Attractions

★ Extensive repertoire of soups such as watercress and ginger, "a nice little green bean soup," cold cucumber cream with yogurt, black bean with lime and an outstanding tortilla soup.

★ A community table where lone diners can avoid eating alone. Lots of friendships and several romantic relationships have developed there.

★ Full service bar. Wine by the glass; 18 wines featured daily and list changes frequently.

★ Afternoon tea.

★ Longtime favorites—Tuesdays are Chicken Fried Steak day and Ouisie's does one of the best chicken-fries anywhere. Thursdays are curry day. Saturdays, look for black beans and rice and Ouisie's exceptional hamburger.

★ Carry-out service for the pimiento cheese, egg salad, house pate, dressings and any menu item. Fresh flowers and Ouisie's blend tea or coffee also for sale.

★ Catering.

★ Art exhibits that change monthly—this month it might be paintings, next month, quilts, photographs, rugs or masks.

★ Rocking chairs on the front "porch."

Grilled Tuna Ouisie With Gremalotta

4   slices bacon, cut in pieces
4   tomatoes, peeled, seeded and cut into chunks
2   cloves garlic, pressed or minced
1   white onion, thinly sliced
    Zest and juice of 1 lemon
    Butter
¼   teaspoon white pepper or more as desired
    Fresh basil, tarragon and oregano (about 1 tablespoon each)
½   cup white wine
½   cup fish fumet (stock)
6   ounces fresh tuna
    Marinated lemon slices (see note)
    Garnishes
    Gremalotta (Italian condiment)

Fry bacon pieces in large pan with tomato chunks, garlic, onion, lemon zest and juice. Work in a little butter. Season to taste with white pepper and herbs.

Add white wine and let simmer a few minutes to reduce and develop flavors. Add fish fumet.

Grill tuna over charcoal grill, basting with olive oil, about 2 minutes on each side, no more than 6 minutes in all. Do not overcook.

To Serve: In shallow glass bowl, pour ½ cup sauce. Top with grilled tuna. Garnish with a marinated lemon slice, 2 anchovies, Greek olives, sprinkle of capers and gremalotta.

Gremalotta
1 teaspoon each per serving: grated lemon peel, finely chopped garlic and finely chopped cilantro

Mound 1 teaspoon of each on plate next to tuna.

Note: Slice lemons very thinly. Marinate in olive oil, basil and white pepper for at least an hour, but preferably overnight. They will keep in the refrigerator for quite a while. Bring to room temperature before using.

Shrimp Acapulco

This was created by Deschaune Bellamy, one of the day cooks at Ouisie's.

2   tomatoes, finely diced
1   white onion, finely diced
3   large jalapenos, seeded and finely diced (leave some of the ribs)
1   bunch cilantro, chopped
½   cup fresh lime juice
    Salt to taste
1   pound peeled shrimp
    Cumin (ground cominos)
1   tablespoon pureed garlic
5   ears fresh corn, cut from the cob
    Avocado oil or other light oil
½   cup combined white wine and fish fumet
    Juice of 1 lime
    Mexican rice
4   ounces (1 cup) shredded Monterey Jack cheese
    Guacamole, sour cream and chopped cilantro for garnish

Make pico de gallo: Combine diced tomatoes, onion, jalapenos, cilantro, lime juice and salt. Refrigerate in covered container.

Lightly dust shrimp with cumin. Saute shrimp, garlic and corn in avocado oil until shrimp are pink.

Add ⅓ cup pico de gallo and simmer a few minutes. Add ½ cup combined white wine and fish fumet and lime juice and simmer until shrimp are done.

Serve over Mexican Rice (brown rice in skillet with onions and fresh coarsely chopped jalapenos, then cook, adding strands of saffron to the boiling water).

Top with shredded cheese and run under broiler until cheese melts slightly.

Garnish with a dollop of guacamole and sour cream and chopped cilantro.

Serves 4.

Serve extra pico de gallo on the side. Leftover pico de gallo can be used in vinaigrette dressing, stir-fry dishes and soup.

Stuffed Pork Tenders

  2   (14- to 16-ounce) boneless pork tenders
 2½   cups chopped fresh spinach
  2   tablespoons chopped shallots
      Zest of peel of 2 oranges
  3   tablespoons chopped fresh basil
  2   tablespoons chopped Italian parsley
 ⅓   cup lightly toasted pine nuts (pignolia)
 ¼   cup breadcrumbs (French bread
      preferred)
  1   egg
 ⅓   cup raisins (can use golden), plumped
      in rum or brandy
  1   teaspoon pureed garlic
 ¼   teaspoon salt and pepper
      Bacon strips
      Plum or apricot jam thinned with
      brandy or rum

Slice pork tenders down the middle about three-fourths of the way through. Place between sheets of plastic wrap and pound out to flatten.

Make Spinach Filling: Saute spinach and shallots in a little butter. Combine with orange zest, basil, parsley, pine nuts, breadcrumbs, egg, raisins, garlic, salt and pepper.

Place filling down the middle of tenders. Roll up and tie with kitchen string.

To roast: Place tenders on rack in pan and lay bacon strips over top. Roast at 350 or 375 degrees until done, 40 to 50 minutes. Glaze the last 5 minutes with plum or apricot jam thinned with brandy or rum.

Let sit about 15 minutes, then clip string and slice. Serve 3 slices per person. Excellent served at room temperature.

Serves 6 to 8.

Roasted Red Bell Peppers With Bacon and Cheese Sandwich

2   red bell peppers, roasted, peeled and cored
12 slices bacon, cooked crisp (Italian pancetta or peppered bacon recommended)
½   pound fresh Mozzarella cheese, sliced
    Pesto Mayonnaise*
    Grated or shaved Parmesan cheese
    Black pepper
8   slices pumpernickel, sourdough or Italian bread

Prepare peppers and bacon; slice Mozzarella (2 ounces per serving).

Spread Pesto Mayonnaise on two slices of bread.

For each sandwich, on one slice of bread layer 3 slices bacon, half a roasted pepper and 2 ounces Mozzarella. Sprinkle Parmesan and pepper over top and place under broiler until cheese is melted. Top with second slice of bread.

*To your favorite mayonnaise, add pesto or minced garlic and chopped fresh basil to taste.

Makes 4.

Garlic Mashed Potatoes

Wonderful with roast chicken and sauteed wild mushrooms, says Ouisie's owner Elouise Cooper.

4   California potatoes, peeled, cut in chunks, cooked until tender and drained
¼   pound unsalted butter, softened
    Salt and pepper to taste
1   tablespoon pureed garlic
1   cup heavy (whipping) cream
    Buttered breadcrumbs

Puree potatoes, butter, salt, pepper, garlic and cream in food processor. Work quickly so mixture does not become sticky.

Pour into buttered shallow baking dish and sprinkle with breadcrumbs. Bake at 350 degrees until heated through.

Serves 4.

Vegetarian Variation #1

2   leeks, julienned with a little of the green tops
1   red bell pepper, grilled and cut into strips
2   tablespoons butter
1   teaspoon pureed garlic
1   cup broth (chicken, beef, fish or vegetable)
3   tablespoons fresh herbs (combination of parsley, basil, oregano, etc.)
     Salt and pepper to taste
2   ounces white wine
4   mushroom caps
1   bunch fresh spinach
     Lemon Ginger Rice (recipe follows)
4   Belgian endive (see note)
2   hard-cooked eggs
     Freshly grated Parmesan cheese

Saute leeks and pepper strips in butter with pureed garlic.

Add broth, herbs, salt, peper and wine. Add mushroom caps and simmer a few minutes.

Add spinach and cook just long enough to wilt. Serve over Lemon Ginger Rice and top with one mushroom cap, braised endive and a hard-cooked egg half. Pass Parmesan at the table.

Serves 4.

Note: To braise endive, arrange in baking dish, add chicken stock to about half way up depth of endive, dot with butter and sprinkle with salt and pepper. Bake covered with foil in 350-degree oven until soft, about 30 minutes. Remove foil and let brown last 5 minutes.

Lemon Ginger Rice

Ouisie's owner Elouise Cooper attributes this recipe to talented cooking teacher Suneeta Vaswani.

⅛   teaspoon saffron threads
2⅝   cups boiling water
1   cup Basmati rice, washed and drained (use Indian or Texmati rice)
1   teaspoon salt
⅛   cup oil
1½   teaspoons finely chopped ginger
½   teaspoon black mustard seeds
2   whole cloves
½   serrano pepper, finely chopped
1½   tablespoons finely chopped cilantro
¼   cup fresh lemon juice
⅛   cup finely grated unsweetened coconut

Soak saffron 10 minutes in ⅛ cup boiling water. Preheat oven to 350 degrees.

Meanwhile, bring 2 cups water to a boil in a large saucepan. Stirring constantly, add rice slowly to water so it does not stop boiling. Add ½ teaspoon salt and cook briskly, uncovered, over medium heat about 10 minutes. Strain and set aside.

In a large casserole (which has a tight-fitting lid), heat oil over high heat until a drop of water flicked into it sputters immediately.

Add ginger, mustard seeds and cloves. Stirring constantly, fry until the seeds begin to crackle and burst.

Stirring well after each addition, add remaining ½ teaspoon salt, serrano pepper, rice, cilantro, lemon juice, coconut and remaining ½ cup boiling water.

Sprinkle saffron and its water over the top and bring to a boil over high heat, stirring occasionally.

Cover pan with foil, crimping edges to hold it firmly in place. Set the lid securely on top of the foil and bake in the middle of the oven 25 minutes. Fluff rice with a fork and serve.

Serves 4.

Negre en Chemise

Cooper got the recipe for this dense, rich chocolate dessert from an English friend in London. The digestive biscuits are a plain, lightly sweetened cookie like a baby's arrowroot biscuit. They often come in decorative tins.

1   package plain English "digestive" biscuits, crumbled fairly finely but not ground to a powder

6   ounces (1½ sticks) unsalted butter, melted

1   cup heavy (whipping) cream

14 ounces chocolate chips

2   egg yolks

4   tablespoons each rum and brandy

Work cookie crumbs into melted butter in a heavy frying pan to form a firm, moist paste. Turn into a buttered 9-inch pie pan.

Press and push the paste to form a firm crust, bringing up the sides to the rim of the pan. Chill until firmly set. Spread 2 ounces stiffly whipped cream over the base and make the filling.

Soften chocolate chips over hot water (or in microwave on low power; stir to smooth), beat thoroughly and when absolutely smooth and runny, quickly beat in egg yolks, rum and brandy.

Beat again, then beat in remaining cream. Spread quickly over cream. Serve in small slices because it is very dense and rich. Top with a dollop of unsweetened whipped cream.

Ouisie's
1708 Sunset Blvd.
Houston, 77005
528-2264

Peng's

FAVORITES

General Tso's Chicken
Peng's Special Beef
Eggplant in Garlic Sauce
Fried Noodles with 10 Ingredients

In this elegant restaurant just west of the Galleria area, Houstonians can enjoy Hunan cuisine as created by celebrated Chinese chef C.K. Peng.

He was born in Changsha, the capital of Hunan province. Now 72, he lives in Taiwan but periodically visits Houston where his eldest son, Chuck Peng, operates Peng's of Houston.

Chef Peng created his palate-warming Haute Hunan cuisine in the 1950s when he was personal chef for then-president of the Republic of China Chiang Kai-shek. Peng apprenticed at 13 with the chef of the first premier of the Chinese Republic. Many of the dishes were created for state banquets honoring distinguished guests such as President Franklin Roosevelt and other heads of state.

The Houston restaurant, specializes in banquet feasts of six to twelve courses, smaller parties and family meals.

Chuck Peng designed the waterfall fountain that occupies one wall of the dining room. The setting is enhanced by mirrored columns and a reproduction of an antique eight-panel gold-leafed screen, both made in Taipei. Peng also designed the rose velvet-upholstered chairs with bentwood arms. Arched half-moons, some opening to private dining alcoves, are draped with Burgundy velvet and bamboo-pattern lace curtains. Swagged crystal chandeliers cast shimmering light patterns on the ceiling.

Peng's culinary honor roll includes General Tso's Prawns, large shrimp sauteed in a ginger-garlic sauce; honey-glazed walnuts, honey Hunan ham, honey-roasted Beggar's Chicken and Water Chestnut Cake, a dessert.

Perhaps the master chef's most famous dish is Lobster Double Soong, created for the opening of the first Peng's in the United States. It is doubly unusual because salads are not common in Chinese meals.

Star Attractions

★ Refined setting. The two solid marble fu dogs guarding the entrance weigh 5,000 pounds and are said to be the heaviest ever shipped to the U.S. A 3,000-pound solid marble Happy Buddha sits in the entry (pat his tummy for good luck). Framed antique Chinese handwriting samples are a unique art object in one dining room.

★ Elaborate banquet-style dishes so artistically arranged they are like edible paintings on the plate. Under Peng's chefs' skilled hands, winter melons are carved into decorative baskets used as serving containers for some dishes and vegetables become flowers used as colorful garnishes.

★ Crispy honeyed walnuts served as an appetizer.

★ Free home or office delivery seven days a week within a five-mile radius.

★ Catering. Peng's can handle everything from dinner for six to formal banquets for several hundred.

★ Private rooms for small or large parties such as wedding receptions.

★ Banquets done with correct Chinese protocol for business entertaining.

★ A rare (and extremely potent) Chinese liquor called moutai, made from wheat. Its use dates from the early 1700s.

General Tso's Chicken

- 1   whole chicken (see note)
- 2   whole eggs (or whites only)
-     Cornstarch
- ½ teaspoon salt
-     Light soy sauce
- 1   tablespoon sugar
- 2   teaspoons rice wine vinegar
- 1   tablespoon minced garlic
- 1   tablespoon minced ginger
-     Chicken broth
-     Peanut Oil
- 1   dried red chile pepper
-     Sesame oil
- 1   green onion, finely chopped or sliced

Remove chicken legs and thighs. Bone and cut meat into 2x1-inch chunks; set aside.

Make a broth with the rest of the chicken: Place chicken in a deep saucepan, cover with water and season to taste; boil until tender. Remove chicken, bone and use for another purpose.

Marinate chicken leg and thigh chunks in a mixture of beaten eggs, 2 tablespoons cornstarch, salt and ½ cup soy sauce. For a more delicate batter, use beaten egg whites only.

Meanwhile, prepare the sauce: Mix ½ cup soy sauce, sugar, vinegar, garlic, ginger, 1 tablespoon cornstarch and ¼ cup chicken broth.

Heat 1 quart peanut oil in a wok over a high heat or in deep-fat fryer until small bubbles appear on the surface (oil should be just below the smoking point). Add chicken and deep-fry 30 seconds.

Remove chicken and reheat oil to original temperature. Return chicken to pan and deep-fry another 20 seconds or until chicken turns golden. Crust should be slightly crunchy. Drain well.

Pour oil off and discard or save for another use. Heat 1 tablespoon fresh peanut oil in wok. Add dry chile pepper and stir-fry 10 seconds.

Return chicken to wok with sauce and stir quickly to coat. Add ¼ teaspoon sesame oil and green onion. Serve immediately.

Serves 2 to 4 depending on number of other dishes served.

Note: Boned chicken legs and thighs and previously homemade or canned chicken stock may be used instead of whole chicken. Be sure oil is maintained at proper temperature so chicken will not absorb oil and become greasy. Oil should sizzle when chicken is added.

Peng's Special Beef

½   cup plus 1 tablespoon cornstarch
    Black pepper
¼   teaspoon salt
2   eggs
¼   teaspoon baking powder
½   pound beef tenderloin, cut into
    2x1x½-inch strips
1½ teaspoons rice wine vinegar
2½ teaspoons sugar
1½ tablespoons ketchup
¾   teaspoon hot pepper oil
1½ teaspoons minced garlic
1½ tablespoons hoisin sauce
2   tablespoons chicken broth
½   cup flour
    Peanut oil
2   cups water
¼   teaspoon sesame oil

Make a marinade by combining 1 tablespoon cornstarch, ½ teaspoon black pepper, salt, 1 egg and baking powder. Place beef strips in bowl with marinade, stirring to coat well. Marinate 10 to 30 minutes.

For sauce: Mix vinegar, sugar, ketchup, hot pepper oil, ⅓ teaspoon black pepper, minced garlic, hoisin sauce and chicken broth.

For batter: Whisk together flour, ½ cup cornstarch, 1 tablespoon peanut oil, remaining egg and water. Remove beef from marinade with strainer, drain and coat with batter.

Heat 1 quart peanut oil in wok until small bubbles appear at the top of the oil. It should be just under the smoking point. Deep-fry beef in small batches (so beef strips won't stick together) 30 seconds each. Drain beef with a strainer.

Reheat oil to original temperature, return beef to oil and fry another 30 seconds. Remove beef and drain again. Discard oil in wok or save for another use.

Coat wok with 1 tablespoon fresh peanut oil. Pour in the sauce and add fried beef. Stir-fry until beef is brown. A good coating should have developed on beef.

Add sesame oil and stir-fry 10 seconds more. Serve immediately.

Serves 2 to 4 depending on number of other dishes served.

Eggplant in Garlic Sauce

1   eggplant, peeled and cut in
    2x½x½-inch pieces
1   piece ginger root (mince 1½ teaspoons;
    shred 1½ teaspoons)
1   tablespoon plus ½ teaspoon sherry
    wine
5   tablespoons rice wine vinegar
5   tablespoons sugar
1   tablespoon soy sauce
    Peanut oil
4   to 6 cloves garlic, minced
⅛   pound shredded pork
2   green onions, cut in 1-inch pieces
1½ teaspoons hot chile pepper sauce
1   teaspoon sesame oil

Prepare sauce: Mix 1½ teaspoons minced ginger, sherry, vinegar, sugar and soy sauce. Set aside.

Heat 1 quart peanut oil in wok until little bubbles appear on the surface (temperature should be just under the smoking point). Deep-fry eggplant pieces 30 seconds.

Remove eggplant, drain and set aside. Discard oil in wok.

Coat wok with 1 tablespoon fresh oil. Put 1½ teaspoons shredded ginger, minced garlic, shredded pork and green onion into wok. Stir quickly a few seconds.

Add ginger-sherry sauce and pepper sauce. Saute 40 seconds. Add sesame oil. Serve immediately.

Serves 2 to 4 depending on number of other dishes served.

Fried Noodles with 10 Ingredients

This is an easy way to express your own creativity in Chinese cooking. Use leftovers, your own favorite 10 ingredients or the following ingredients in proportions to suit your taste. Chuck Peng says any type of soft noodles can be used—Chinese noodles or even spaghetti.

	Sliced chicken pieces
	Shrimp
	Oil
	Sliced ham
¼	**head napa (Chinese cabbage)**
	Snow peas (6 or to taste)
	Broccoli florets
	Baby corn
	Straw mushrooms
	Bamboo shoots
	Sliced water chestnuts
1	**package soft Chinese noodles or other noodles, cooked**
2	**tablespoons soy sauce**
½	**teaspoon sugar**
	Green onions cut in small pieces
½	**teaspoon black pepper**
1	**teaspoon sesame oil**

In wok, deep-fry the chicken in oil until it turns white. Deep-fry shrimp (do not overcook). Remove chicken and shrimp from oil, drain and set aside. Discard oil in wok.

Coat wok with 1 tablespoon fresh oil. Add chicken, shrimp, ham, shredded cabbage, snow peas, broccoli, baby corn, mushrooms, bamboo shoots and water chestnuts. Stir-fry 30 seconds.

Add noodles by the handful; add soy sauce, sugar and scallions. Stir-fry very well. Add pepper and sesame oil. Serve immediately.

Peng's
5923 Westheimer
Houston,
266-1825

Rotisserie for Beef and Bird

The Rotisserie for Beef and Bird offers a dining adventure in American history and a preview of things to come. Under the knowledgeable guidance of chef-proprietor Joe Mannke, early American and Texas regional foods and cooking techniques—charcoal broiling and grilling—are rediscovered and elevated to epicurean status.

An open charcoal hearth and rotisserie are the focal point of the American colonial restaurant in far southwest Houston. Clean-lined architecture, used brick walls and fireplaces, flowers in planter boxes, handmade parqueted oak tables, brass coach lamps and captain's chairs extend a warm welcome.

Mannke couples years of experience as a hotel and restaurant chef in Europe, South Africa and the U.S. with an innate sense of true Texas hospitality. He was executive chef at Anthony's Pier 4 in Boston when it became the largest-volume restaurant in the U.S., and as chef in charge of Disney World's seven kitchens when it opened, he supervised the serving of more than 10,000 meals a day.

He is a member of the Confrerie de la Chaine des Rotisseurs, Les Amis d'Escoffier and American Academy of Chefs. The Rotisserie opened in 1978 and has been almost reservations-required ever since. It has won numerous awards including the Travel Holiday award every year since 1981 and the award of excellence form The Wine Spectator in 1986.

Only the finest, freshest foods are used, and they are treated with respect. Menus feature fine beef, duck, chicken, Gulf Coast oysters, shrimp and crab, New England lobster, farm-fresh vegetables and freshly baked breads and desserts. The wine list includes more than 500 selections.

Star Attractions

★ American food, attentive service and concern for details such as crisp salads. Specialties such as world-class steak tartare (not on menu), pate, homemade rolls and ice creams.

★ Skillfully prepared Texas wild game such as tender medallions of Axis deer sauteed in brown butter, mesquite-grilled loin of wild boar with a subtle plum sauce, roast pheasant with grapes and pine nuts, mesquite-grilled Hill Country partridge and pan-fried quails.

★ Exceptional wine list, one of the best in the city—more than 500 fairly priced selections and an inventory of 16,000 bottles.

★ Beautifully appointed wine cellar for private parties.

★ Cozy library-like bar with fireplace. Complimentary pate and cheese spreads.

★ Traditional America the Plentiful feast at Thanksgiving.

★ Mouthwatering desserts—Jack Daniels Chocolate Chip Ice Cream with Sticky Pecans, Bread Pudding With Hot Whiskey Sauce, Praline Ice Cream Pie with Chocolate Hazelnut Sauce.

Bisque of Butternut Squash and Apples

1½   pounds peeled, seeded butternut or other hard-shell squash
2   tart green apples, peeled and chopped
1   onion, coarsely chopped
    Pinch each of rosemary and marjoram
½   teaspoon salt
2   teaspoons brown sugar
¼   teaspoon white pepper
1   quart chicken stock (preferably homemade)
½   stick (4 tablespoons) butter
2   tablespoons flour
2   egg yolks
1½   cups half-and-half

Combine the squash, chopped apples, onion, herbs, salt, sugar, pepper and chicken stock in a heavy saucepan. Bring to a boil and simmer about 1 hour.

Scoop the squash and apples out of the soup, puree in electric blender and return to soup.

In a separate saucepan, melt butter. Add flour, mix well and strain the soup over the flour mixture, a little at a time. Stir well with a whisk; bring to a boil.

In a small bowl, beat egg yolks and half-and-half together. Beat in a little of the hot soup, then stir back into the saucepan. Heat through, but do not boil.

Serves 6.

Linguine and Fresh Seafood in a Spicy Sauce

2   (10 ounce) cans beef consomme
2   bay leaves
1   (3-ounce) pouch crab boil
4   tablespoons butter
½   onion, peeled and chopped
3   cloves garlic, chopped
1   teaspoon paprika
3   tablespoons flour
1   teaspoon tomato paste
½   cup heavy (whipping) cream
¼   teaspoon black pepper
1   pound linguine
½   pound small shrimp, peeled and deveined
½   pound fresh crabmeat
6   ounces scallops, cooked
½   cup freshly grated Parmesan cheese
6   mussels, cooked, for garnish (optional)

Bring the consomme, bay leaves and crab boil (leave spices in the pouch) to a boil in a large pot; simmer 10 minutes.

Melt 2 tablespoons butter in a heavy saucepan and saute onion and garlic until light brown. Stir in paprika and flour and combine with tomato paste.

Remove from range carefully, so you don't puncture the crab boil pouch, strain the consomme over the flour mixture and bring to a boil. Whisk until sauce is smooth. Strain and combine with cream and black pepper.

In the meantime, boil the linguine in large pot of boiling water, until soft but still firm.

Saute shrimp, crabmeat and scallops in remaining butter in a skillet. Mix with sauce, then combine with linguine. Top with Parmesan. Garnish with mussels, if desired.

Serves 6.

Grilled Shrimp and Chicken on Brochette

1   (2-pound) chicken, cut up, or 1 pound boneless, skinned chicken breast
1   pound large (12-count) shrimp, peeled and deveined
    Marinade
2   green peppers
1   medium onion

With sharp knife remove the two halves of the chicken breast by cutting through the center of the chicken. Remove the legs.

Cut out the leg bones and discard all skin. Cut chicken into 1½-inch pieces. Marinate chicken and shrimp overnight in marinade.

Cut green peppers in half, seed, then cut in 1½-inch pieces. Peel onion, cut in half, then in 1½-inch pieces.

Alternate chicken, shrimp, peppers and onion on a large brochette or divide among 6 skewers. Cook to desired doneness on mesquite grill over hot coals, about 25 minutes, turning occasionally. Serve over rice.

Serves 6.

Marinade
1   cup light soy sauce
½   cup honey
1   teaspoon ginger
½   teaspoon black pepper
8   cloves garlic, finely chopped
⅓   cup sherry wine

Whisk marinade ingredients together; pour over chicken and shrimp.

Medallions of Veal with Julienne of Vegetables and Cheese

12   (3-ounce) veal medallions, thinly sliced
1   cup each: julienned carrots, leeks, zucchini and cabbage
    Salt and pepper
½   cup all-purpose flour
1   stick (8 tablespoons) butter
1   cup heavy (whipping) cream
    Pinch of marjoram
½   cup freshly grated Parmesan cheese
    Pinch of paprika
6   slices Swiss cheese

Drop julienned vegetable strips into rapidly boiling water to blanch, about 2 to 3 minutes, drain, then rinse with cold water. While vegetables are cooking, pound the medallions thin, season with salt and pepper and dust with flour.

Melt butter in large frying pan. Saute veal quickly over high heat until golden brown. Arrange side by side on an ovenproof serving platter. Keep warm.

Bring cream to a boil, add marjoram and Parmesan and simmer until lightly thickened. Combine with vegetables and mound on each medallion.

Cover each with thinly sliced Swiss cheese, sprinkle with paprika and bake in (400-degree) oven 5 minutes or until cheese starts to melt.

Serves 6.

Diet Alert: Reduce butter to 4 tablespoons or substitute diet margarine or spray pan with non-stick spray. Substitute milk or evaporated skim milk for cream, reduce Parmesan to ¼ cup and use low-fat cheese for Swiss.

Poached Fresh Pears With Zabaglione Sauce

6   large pears with stems, peeled
1½ quarts (6 cups) red wine
6   whole cloves
2   cinnamon sticks
1   cup sugar
    Zabaglione Sauce

Select large, firm pears, peel and core from the bottom leaving a ¾-inch hole. Bring the wine, cloves, cinnamon sticks and sugar to a boil in a large saucepan.

Place pears in the wine and simmer until tender; be careful not to overcook.

Let pears cool in the wine, drain and place each in a long stem glass. To serve: Pour Zabaglione Sauce over pears. Garnish as desired.

Zabaglione Sauce
5   egg yolks
1   cup dry white wine
    Juice of 1 lemon
½   cup sugar
    Pinch of powdered sugar

Beat egg yolks and whisk in wine, lemon juice, sugar and powdered sugar.

Place in the top of a double boiler over simmering, but not boiling, water. Beat with a wire whisk until light and frothy. Serve immediately.

Diet Alert: Serve pears with some of the cooking juices instead of Zabaglione Sauce.

Rotisserie for Beef and Bird
2200 Wilcrest
Houston, 77042
977-9524

Ruggles Grille

FAVORITES

Snapper and Crab Chowder

*Black Pepper Pasta with
Sweet Garlic Cream and Chicken*

*Warm Grilled Chicken Salad with
Roquefort and Walnuts*

*Grilled Red Snapper with
Spicy Crawfish Salsa*

Blanca's Strawberry Cream Roll

R uggles, opened by restaurateur Manfred Jachmich in a remodeled old house in 1974, was an early fixture on the neartown Westheimer strip. It is currently enjoying a renaissance under the leadership of talented and promising young chef/owner Bruce Molzan.

The setting remains casual and open—stained glass windows from an old English pub, gray walls and white woodwork, antiques, striped banquettes and plants in hanging baskets.

Molzan trained briefly with Wolfgang Puck whose influence is present in such menu items as pizza and pasta. Old favorites such as Manfred's Trout Meuniere are still on the menu, but Molzan makes his own culinary statement with dishes such as Spicy Grilled Fish with Crawfish Salsa and Sesame Catfish, Abbas' Crabby Cakes, Warm Grilled Chicken Salad with Roquefort and Toasted Walnuts and Onion Soup El Paso.

Born in Virginia, he is the son of a retired naval officer; the family lived and traveled all over the U.S. Molzan is a graduate of the Culinary Institute of America and started his career as a dishwasher at 15. He worked his way up to butcher and cook and came to Houston after graduation in 1982.

He was with a hotel chain briefly, worked under chef Herve Glin at the former Warwick Post Oak for two years, then became chef at a new disco and club, SRO, since closed.

While there he was sent to California for a short time to work at Spago with Puck who was doing French Nouvelle cooking with California ingredients.

Molzan's experiences there inspired him to develop his own regional style and seasonal menus using fresh local ingredients—such as honey-roasted Texas onions with grilled veal liver, fresh Gulf Coast red snapper and crab in chowder and spicy chicken sausage topping for pizza.

Star Attractions

★ Inventive chef, contemporary cooking. Specialties include Fried Texas Mozzarella and Zucchini with Mustard Sauce, Buffalo Chicken Wings, Homemade Onion Rings, Grilled Lamb T-Bone Chops With Peppered Port Wine Sauce and desserts made in the Ruggles kitchen.

★ Menu well-balanced with fresh fish, beef, chicken, seafood, sandwiches and burgers. Chef's favorites and house specialties are starred in red.

★ Moderte prices. Casual upbeat atmosphere.

★ Sunday brunch with a harpist. The menu features egg and pasta dishes, Almond French Toast, grilled specialties and Blackened Catfish with Shrimp.

★ Small, but thoughtfully chosen wine list that leans to French and California selections. Chef's favorites are marked in red.

★ On request, the chef can accommodate special diet needs, such as cooking without fat or omitting sauces.

★ Private rooms for small parties.

Ruggles Snapper and Crab Chowder

This is chef Bruce Molzan's answer to gumbo. He wanted to offer gumbo at Ruggles and began asking friends for their recipes, but they were so contradictory, he soon realized that gumbo is too personal a regional dish. Because he is from Virginia where chowder is a native dish, he decided to add it to the menu instead. It's now one of his most popular signature dishes.

1	gallon water
5	pounds fish bones
½	cup each oil and flour for roux
1	cup chopped onion
3	tablespoons chopped garlic
¼	cup olive oil
1	cup chopped celery
1	cup each chopped red and yellow bell peppers
6	jalapenos, chopped
2	cups peeled, seeded, chopped tomatoes
3½	cups tomato juice
1	teaspoon each dried basil, oregano and thyme
4	bay leaves
1	bunch cilantro, chopped Freshly ground black pepper and salt to taste
1	pound Italian sausage, sliced into ¼-inch rounds
2	(8-ounce) red snapper fillets, cut into 1-inch squares
2	(8-ounce) catfish fillets
1	pound crabmeat
1	pound shrimp, peeled and deveined
2	chicken breasts, skinned and cut into 1-inch squares or 1 whole fryer, cut up, skinned and boned

Prepare stock by simmering bones in water 30 minutes. Strain and reserve.

Make a roux: Heat oil in small saucepan. Whisk in flour and simmer over medium heat, stirring constantly, until light brown, 15 to 20 minutes. Roux does not have to be as dark as the traditional roux for Cajun gumbo. Reserve and let cool.

In a large soup kettle, saute onion and garlic in olive oil until vegetables are transparent, about 10 minutes. Add celery, peppers and tomatoes; saute 10 minutes more.

Add stock and tomato juice and simmer about 1 hour. Add reserved, cooled roux, herbs and half the cilantro (reserve the rest to garnish each serving). Season to taste with pepper and salt and simmer 30 minutes.

Add sausage and cook 10 minutes. Add fish fillets, crab, shrimp and chicken and let simmer another 30 minutes.

Skim off any fat rendered by sausage. Serve as an appetizer or main course garnished with wedge of lime or lemon and a sprinkling of chopped cilantro.

Freezes well.

Serves 8 to 10 generously.

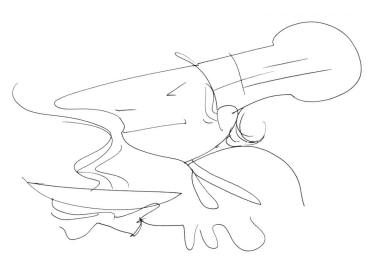

Black Pepper Pasta with Sweet Garlic Cream and Chicken

4   quarts water
¾   pound black pepper pasta (available at fresh pasta shops such as Ferrari Fresh Pasta)
6   garlic cloves
2   whole chicken breasts, split
     Coarsely ground fresh black pepper
1   cup vermouth
3   cups cream
¼   cup freshly grated Parmesan cheese
⅓   cup each julienned carrots, leeks and zucchini

Bring water to a boil in large pot and cook pasta al dente (firm to the tooth), about 3 or 4 minutes. Drop whole garlic cloves in boiling water and simmer about 5 minutes. Peel, press through a sieve to puree, and reserve.

Applying some pressure, roll chicken breasts in black pepper. Cook, either in oven, saute pan or over grill, until done, about 5 to 7 minutes. Slice into fourths diagonally. Reserve.

Make sauce: Reduce vermouth to 1 tablespoon. Add cream and reduce by half. Add Parmesan and pureed garlic. Thin with chicken stock if necessary. Add julienned vegetables at the last minute and cook another minute or so.

Put cooked pasta in saucepan and toss to coat with sauce. Divide evenly among 4 plates. Place sliced chicken breast over pasta. Serve immediately.

Makes 4 servings.

Warm Grilled Chicken Salad with Roquefort and Walnuts

     Dressing
2   chicken breasts, skinned and boned
     Olive oil
     Chopped parsley and oregano
1   cup each: romaine, red leaf and Boston lettuces and spinach
1   Red Delicious apple, cored, cut into fourths and julienned
1   lemon, cut into 4 wedges
½   cup coarsely chopped toasted walnuts
¼   pound imported Roquefort cheese, cut in 4 sticks

Make dressing: Brush chicken breasts with olive oil and sprinkle with some chopped parsley and oregano. Bake, broil or grill chicken about 5 to 7 minutes. Cut each breast in half. In a large salad bowl, mix greens and toss with dressing.

Place generous serving of greens on 4 salad plates. Arrange julienned apple, ⅛ cup walnuts, a lemon wedge and 1 Roquefort stick by greens. Place chicken breasts next to cheese. Serve immediately while chicken is still warm, or refrigerate and serve chilled.

Serves 4.

Dressing
¼   cup vinegar
2   egg yolks
1   cup chicken stock, reduced to ⅛ cup
1   tablespoon Dijon mustard
1   teaspoon finely chopped fresh parsley
½   teaspoon finely chopped fresh oregano
     Salt and pepper to taste
¾   cup olive oil

Combine vinegar, egg yolks, stock, mustard, parsley, oregano, salt and pepper in a small bowl. Whisk in oil slowly until well incorporated.

Grilled Red Snapper with Spicy Crawfish Salsa

    4   (8 to 10-ounce) red snapper fillets
    2   tablespoons Spicy Oil
         Crawfish Salsa
         Beurre Blanc (white butter)
         Freshly grated Parmesan cheese

Brush fillets with Spicy Oil. Broil or grill about 3 to 4 minutes on each side over high heat. Place fillets on individual plates and scoop a generous portion of Crawfish Salsa beside each. Nap with about 2 tablespoons beurre blanc. Top with grated Parmesan.

Serves 4

Spicy Oil

Add seeds of 6 jalapenos to 1 cup extra-virgin olive oil. Steep 24 hours. Use for marinades or as a seasoning oil for meats and seafoods.

Crawfish Salsa
    4   tomatoes, peeled, seeded and chopped
    3   shallots, finely chopped
    2   jalapenos, seeded and chopped
         Juice of 2 limes
         Juice of 1 lemon
    3   teaspoons olive oil
    ¾   cup boiled crawfish tails
    3   teaspoons chopped cilantro
         Salt and pepper to taste

Combine tomatoes, shallots, jalapenos, juices, oil, crawfish, cilantro, salt and pepper in mixing bowl. Set aside.

Beurre Blanc
    4   shallots, finely chopped
    12   ounces vermouth
         Juice of 2 lemons
         Juice of 1 lime
    2   teaspoons vinegar
    2   cups whipping cream
    ½   pound butter
         Salt and pepper to taste

Combine shallots, vermouth, juices and vinegar in medium saucepan. Reduce to ¼ cup over medium-high heat.

Add cream; reduce by half. Whip in butter by the tablespoon. Salt and pepper to taste. Keep warm, but do not boil. Makes 2½ cups.

The remaining can be frozen. To reuse: Break into cubes. Bring 4 tablespoons whipping cream to a boil and whisk in the frozen cubes.

Blanca's Strawberry Cream Roll

Cake
    4   eggs
    1   cup sugar
    5   tablespoons water
    1   cup all-purpose flour
    1   teaspoon baking powder
    1   teaspoon vanilla extract
         Pinch of salt
         Filling

Grease a large jellyroll pan and line bottom with wax paper. Grease paper and dust with flour.

Beat eggs well in heavy duty electric mixer. Add sugar and beat until creamy. Add water and beat about 15 minutes. Sift flour and baking powder together and add to egg mixture. Add vanilla and salt; beat until smooth.

Pour batter into pan and smooth evenly. Bake at 375 degrees 12 to 15 minutes until cake springs back when lightly touched. Cool completely.

All cake ingredients should be at room temperature.

Strawberry Cream Filling
    3   cups very cold whipping cream
         (also chill bowl and beaters)
    1   cup sifted powdered sugar
    2   teaspoons vanilla
    2   pints fresh strawberries, gently
         washed, patted dry, hulled and sliced

Whip cream, slowly adding sugar and vanilla. Gently fold in sliced strawberries.

Turn cake onto a clean linen towel dusted with powdered sugar. Remove wax paper. Spread filling evenly over cake.

Roll up starting on the long side. Chill before serving. Garnish with fresh strawberries and mint sprigs. Serve in slices.

Ruggles Grill
903 Westheimer
Houston, 77006
524-3839

San Carlos

FAVORITES

Sopes (appetizers)
Tortilla Soup
Chilaquiles (baked casserole of chicken,
chilies and cheese)
Snapper Veracruzana
Mango Mousse

Dining at San Carlos is like a short vacation in Mexico without leaving home. The architecture of the 200-seat restaurant is classic, with tile work, terra cotta, and carved doors, arched doorways and woodwork of dark rustic wood.

Wrought iron grillework in the bar festooned with ivy, plants and flowers, handpainted motifs over windows, and walls and table linens in Mexican peach create a pleasant, appealing background for San Carlos' more sophisticated Mexican food.

The food really presents the best of two worlds—authentic regional Mexican food with a bit of zesty Tex-Mex here and there (Texas favorites are marked with a star on the menu).

San Carlos is the first venture outside Mexico City for the Loredo family, which owns eight highly successful restaurants. Managing partner Carlos Rodriguez, who lives here, says they have made a commitment to Houston and are trying to achieve the same excellence at San Carlos that has made the company a household word in Mexico City.

To expose Houstonians to more unique and traditional Mexican fare they offer such specialties as La Palomilla, sizzling top sirloin with herbs, onions and serrano peppers; Camarones or Huachinango al Ajillo, shrimp or snapper marinated with garlic sauce; chilaquiles, a baked casserole of chicken, chilies and cheese, and Saltillo Tamales with an ancho chile sauce. And always black beans, not pintos. But they also feature an excellent version of that runaway Texas favorite, fajitas.

The emphasis currently is on lighter, more health-conscious dishes. Daily specials change seasonally. The light menu features lots of fish and salads. Popular dishes include chicken salad with apples and pineapple and charbroiled chicken breast topped with chipotle sauce.

Star Attractions

★ A blend of more sophisticated Mexican food and Texas favorites.

★ Attractive setting for special parties, especially wedding rehearsals, weddings and bar mitzvahs.

★ Sopes ("SOAP-ehs"), typical Mexican appetizer tidbits, are a specialty. For parties, they can be made fresh by hand at the tile-countered "Tortilla Shop" in the bar while guests watch.

★ Lively Happy Hour with free buffet of an array of San Carlos specialties.

★ Beef or chicken fajitas presented on sizzling platters of metal and wood with onions, cheese, sauces and black beans in distinctive blue-and-white Tolucan pottery bowls.

★ Home delivery of food via Dial n Dine.

★ Drink specialties including strawberry margaritas, pina coladas served in a decorated pineapple shell, imported Mexican beers and wine by the glass.

Sopes

San Carlos' Botana Tipica appetizer platter includes snack-size chalupas, sopes and tostaditas.

1½ cups masa harina (Mexican corn flour)
1 cup warm water
2 cups refried black beans
1 cup chorizo (remove casing, crumble and fry slowly until fat is rendered)
1 cup shredded Monterey Jack cheese or Queso Blanco (Mexican white cheese)
1 medium onion, finely diced
2 cups shredded lettuce
1 tomato, chopped
Guacamole, pico de gallo and sour cream for garnish

Mix masa harina and water to a soft dough. (If necessary, add a little cooking oil to make dough easier to work with.)

Work dough with your hands and knead until all the water is incorporated and dough is no longer sticky. Set aside while griddle is heating. Lightly oil griddle.

Using about 1 tablespoon masa dough at a time, roll into a 1½-inch ball, then pass it from hand to hand patting it against palms until it flattens into a pancake about 2 inches in diameter and ¼-inch thick (sopes are always thicker than tortillas).

Cook on lightly oiled griddle over medium heat. When done on one side (cake will start to pull up from griddle around edges), turn and quickly cook second side.

Cool slightly then pinch a little ridge around the edge of each to make a saucer-like shell. Return to griddle for a few seconds to rewarm and thoroughly cook centers (some cooks like to put a dab of oil in the center at this point).

Top with beans, chorizo, onion, lettuce, tomato, cheese or desired combination of toppings. Arrange on a platter lined with leaf lettuce. Garnish or serve with guacamole, pico de gallo and sour cream.

San Carlos Tortilla Soup

8 corn tortillas
Oil
2 to 3 tomatoes, cut in chunks
¼ white onion, cut up
1 garlic clove
8 cups chicken broth (preferably homemade)
1 epazote leaf (see note)
Salt and pepper to taste
½ cup grated Monterey Jack cheese
Sour cream
1 pasilla chile
1 avocado (remove seed and cut in slices)

Cut tortillas into 3x½-inch strips. Saute until crisp in a little oil. Drain on paper towels.

Puree tomatoes, onion and garlic in blender or food processor. Fry sauce in 1 tablespoon oil in a saucepan.

Add broth and epazote and salt and pepper to taste. Bring to a boil.

To serve: Place a few tortilla strips in 6 soup bowls and pour broth over them. Add cheese.

Top each with a dollop of sour cream, a piece of chile pasilla and 1 slice of avocado.

Serves 6

Note: Epazote is a weed-like Mexican herb that is sometimes available at Mexican specialty foods stores such as Fiesta. An aromatic plant used as a condiment, it is called "the tea of Mexico."

Chilaquiles

12 to 14 corn tortillas
    Oil
 1 pound tomatillos (Mexican green
    tomatoes with papery husk), peeled,
    cleaned and cut in chunks
 1 clove garlic
 ½ white onion, cut in chunks
 1 tablespoon chopped cilantro
    Salt and pepper to taste
 4 serrano chilies
 ½ chicken breast, cooked in broth and
    shredded
    Sour cream
 ½ cup grated Monterey Jack cheese

Cut tortillas into 2x1-inch strips. Saute in a little hot oil until slightly crisp. Drain on paper towels.

In blender or food processor, make sauce: Puree tomatillos, garlic, onion, cilantro, salt and pepper to taste and chilies.

Fry sauce in 1 tablespoon hot oil 2 to 3 minutes.

Layer in 1½-quart casserole or shallow baking dish: tortilla strips, sauce, chicken, sour cream and cheese; repeat layers.

Bake at 350 degrees until heated thoroughly.

Serves 4

Snapper Veracruzana

The authentic Snapper Veracruz (Huachinango a la Veracruzana) would include capers. San Carlos omits them because they found that most Houston customers have not developed a taste for the piquant capers.

 4 (8 to 10-ounce) fillets of red snapper
    (about 2 pounds)
    Salt and coarsely ground
    black pepper
    Oil
 1 medium onion, thinly sliced
 3 to 4 ripe tomatoes (about 1½ pounds),
    finely chopped (peel if desired)
 1 cup water
 1 Italian green pepper, Cajun pepper
    or jalapeno
 2 garlic cloves, mashed
 1 bay leaf
 1 teaspoon dried oregano
 8 to 10 pimiento-stuffed green olives,
    sliced
    Drained, rinsed capers to taste (optional)

Wash fillets and pat dry. Salt and pepper (also dust with flour if desired). Heat oil in large saute pan and saute fillets until done, turning once. Do not overcook. Set aside and keep warm.

Heat 3 tablespoons oil in large saucepan. Saute onion until translucent. Add chopped tomatoes, water, chopped pepper, salt and freshly ground pepper to taste, garlic, bay leaf and oregano.

Simmer, covered, over medium heat about 5 minutes. Remove bay leaf. Stir in olives the last minute or so.

Place each fillet on a plate and top with sauce (and capers, if desired).

At San Carlos, the fish is accompanied by rice, corn and fresh tomato slices and garnished with parsley.

Serves 4

Mango Mousse

1 pint (2 cups) whipping cream
5 egg yolks
1½ cups sugar
1½ ounces brandy
1 pound fresh mangos, peeled, seeded and pureed

Chill cream, bowl and beaters. Whip egg yolks with ½ cup sugar and the brandy.

Whip cream in chilled bowl with remaining sugar; thoroughly combine with mango puree. Blend cream and egg yolk mixture.

Pour into 8 stemmed crystal glasses or individual dessert dishes. Refrigerate at least 5 hours before serving.

Serves 8

San Carlos
6304 Richmond
Houston 77057
977-2250

Sausalito

FAVORITES

Bammel Garden Salad with Goat Cheese
Ceviche Sausalito
Fettucine Dino
Redfish Aldo
Domenico's Cheesecake

L ight, fresh and flavorful with California flair—that's the food style at Sausalito Restaurant. Co-owner Tomas Romero is from Peru and many of the dishes also reflect his Peruvian background, especially fish and seafood specialties.

Italian, Mediterranean and Mexican flavors also surface now and again, in pasta and other lighthearted seafood dishes.

Some menu items are the creation of longtime staff members such as chef/co-owner Aldo Grubich and chef Willie Dean. Sausalito's best-selling pasta, Fettucine Dino, is named for Dean; the best-selling cheesecake is the namesake of sous chef Domenico Minuta.

Hans Rometsch is the third co-owner of Sausalito, a 100-seat restaurant which opened in 1985 off Westheimer and Kirby Drive in the River Oaks area. The casual setting is in keeping with the menu—comfortable and attractive with a garden room feeling.

The menu has double appeal for the gourmet who is health-conscious. In addition to palate-pleasing beef, chicken and seafood dishes, there are light pastas with fresh vegetable sauces, refreshing salads and a vegetarian platter of the season's best vegetables steamed tender-crisp and served with rice.

Star Attractions

★ Contemporary light California-style cuisine. Fresh pasta by Ferrari. Breads (including a stellar sourdough) baked twice daily for Sausalito by La Madeleine bakery. (Sandwiches are served on the sourdough bread.) Moderate prices.

★ Pasta and salads available in half orders.

★ Unique foods with a Peruvian or regional American touch such as the Peruvian-style Seafood Salad, an intriguing combination of shrimp, baby octopus and baby squid, and one of the best versions of ceviche around, a garlic-pungent presentation of fish chunks "cooked" by marinating in lemon juice.

★ Specialties such as frog legs (a dozen or so regular customers show up every week just for the Frog Legs Pajama, frog legs in a dark Beck's beer batter); Salmon Florentine, grilled salmon on a bed of fresh creamed spinach; Chicken Breast with a Light Peppercorn Brandy Sauce and julienned vegetables, and Chicken Breast a la Grecque with diced fresh tomatoes, leeks and mushrooms.

★ Sunday brunch with a menu of eggs and omelets (Eggs Sausalito is a must). Start the day in a leisurely way with a Mimosa (champagne and orange juice) or Sausalito's outstanding version of the Bloody Mary, or a milkshake.

★ Devastating desserts—few can resist Sausalito's Rum Cake (made for them by Betty Pecore), creamy cheesecake topped with strawberries or amaretto, fresh strawberries drizzled with chocolate or that traditional Texas favorite, pecan ball with Blue Bell homemade vanilla ice cream and homemade hot fudge sauce.

★ A hand-picked wine list of sparkling wines and California award-winners such as Kendall Jackson Chardonnay, Stonegate, Beaulieu, Mondavi, Ridge, Jordan and Rodney Strong. Nice selection of wines by the glass including French and California.

Ceviche Sausalito

1   red onion, thinly sliced
½   teaspoon each salt and white pepper
2   (10-ounce) fish fillets, cut in chunks
     (can use catfish, redfish or other firm
     white-fleshed fish)
½   cup finely chopped celery
¼   cup chopped cilantro
3   serrano peppers, seeded and sliced*
2   garlic cloves, finely chopped
1   cup fresh lemon juice

Soak onion slices in cold water 15 minutes. Drain. Salt and pepper fish.

Mix onion, fish, celery, cilantro, peppers and garlic with lemon juice. Marinate 2 hours at room temperature. The lemon juice "cooks" the fish.

Drain excess marinade. Arrange ceviche on leaf lettuce and garnish with cilantro and lime wedge.

Serves 4.

*Be careful working with hot peppers; they can irritate skin and eyes.

Bammel Garden Salad

This is a signature dish at Sausalito and is one of the most popular salads on the menu.

1   head Boston lettuce, torn into pieces
1   tomato, cut in wedges or sliced
3   whole mushrooms, thinly sliced
1   cup (about) vinaigrette dressing (use
     your favorite recipe or bottled dressing)
     Black olives (imported Calamata olives
     recommended)
6   ounces goat cheese

Toss lettuce, tomato wedges and mushrooms lightly with just enough vinaigrette dressing to coat.

Arrange on 4 salad plates, top with olives and crumbled goat cheese.

Serves 4.

Diet Alert: Use low-calorie vinaigrette.

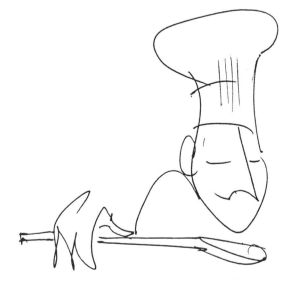

Redfish Aldo

4   (8-ounce) redfish fillets
1   cup chicken broth
    Juice of ½ lemon
    Salt and pepper
¼   cup chopped fresh parsley
½   green leek top, julienned
1   carrot, julienned

Combine broth, lemon juice, salt and pepper to taste, chopped parsley, leek and carrot and bring to a boil in a large skillet.

Carefully place fish in boiling stock. Simmer just long enough to cook, about 5 to 8 minutes.

Remove fish from broth. Arrange on plate.

Serve topped with steamed vegetables and new potatoes.

Serves 4.

Fettucine Dino

One of Sausalito's most popular dishes.

2   fresh tomatoes, chopped
2   ounces (4 tablespoons) butter, melted
    Salt and pepper to taste
1   tablespoon fresh chopped basil
1   quart half-and-half
    Fettucine pasta for 4

Saute tomatoes in melted butter. Add salt, pepper, basil and half-and-half. Bring to a boil.

Cook the pasta: For 1 pound of pasta, bring 4 quarts water to a rolling boil in a large pot. Let boil for a few minutes, then add 1 tablespoon oil and 1 tablespoon salt. Add the pasta all at once and stir with a wooden fork to separate strands. Let boil several minutes until al dente ("firm to the tooth"); test with one strand of pasta. Fresh fettucine takes only a few minutes.

Drain in a large colander and return to pot. Add 1 to 2 tablespoons margarine or butter. Mix with sauce. Serve immediately.

Serves 4.

Chicken Breast a la Grecque

2   pounds chicken breast halves, skinned, boned and grilled
1   small leek, chopped (including green top)
2   cups sliced mushrooms
1   tomato, diced
    Butter
    Salt and pepper
1   cup dry white wine
    Juice of ½ lemon

Grill one (5 to 8-ounce) chicken breast per person over charcoal (or broil or saute).

Combine chopped leek, mushrooms and tomato and saute in a little butter. Salt and pepper to taste. Add wine and lemon juice and simmer a few minutes until vegetables are softened somewhat.

Place chicken breast on plate and top with sauteed vegetables. Serve with boiled new potatoes and a small bouquet of steamed or sauteed vegetables such as carrots, zucchini, yellow squash, cauliflower and green beans.

Serves 4.

Domenico's Cheesecake

The creation of a chef at Tomas Romero's former restaurant, Domenico's Cheesecake is a perennial favorite at Sausalito. It is served topped with strawberries or a jigger of amaretto liqueur.

Crust

1½   cups graham cracker crumbs
1   cup chopped pecans
½   cup melted unsalted butter

Set oven at 350 degrees. Combine cracker crumbs, pecans and butter and press evenly over bottom of 14x10-inch or 13x9x2-inch pan.

Filling

1½   pounds cream cheese, softened to room temperature
4   eggs
3½   cups sugar
1   tablespoon lemon juice

To softened cream cheese, add eggs, sugar and lemon juice. Mix until creamy. Pour over crust.

Set cheesecake on the middle rack of the oven. Bake until firm, about 20 to 25 minutes at 350 degrees. Remove from oven. Let cool a few minutes, then run knife around edge to separate cake from sides of pan. Spread topping over cheesecake while it is still hot.

Topping

1½   pints (3 cups) sour cream
½   cup sugar
1   tablespoon lemon juice

Mix sour cream, sugar and lemon juice in electric mixer until smooth, about 5 minutes. Spread lightly over cheesecake while it is still hot. Let sit 20 minutes, then refrigerate.

Serves 18.

Diet Alert: Substitute diet margarine for butter in crust and reduce nuts to ½ cup. In filling, use light cream cheese or Neufchatel, use 2 whole eggs plus 4 egg whites and reduce sugar to 3 cups. In topping, substitute plain non-fat yogurt for sour cream and reduce sugar to ¼ cup, or use sugar substitute.

Sausalito
3215 Westheimer
Houston, 77005
529-6959

Taste of Texas

FAVORITES

Tortilla Soup
Mushrooms in Butter
Butter Sauce for Sizzling Steaks
Taste of Texas Cornbread
Cinnamon Slammer
Cinnamon Coffee

If you ask owner Edd C. Hendee who created his menu and who is responsible for his restaurant's personality and success, he says, without skipping a beat, "my customers."

That's why, in the past three years, Taste of Texas has forsaken the chicken fried steak for more contemporary food that appeals to computer generation restaurantgoers. (The chicken fried steak was ceremoniously buried in a flower bed at the side of the restaurant under an RIP headstone.)

Hendee inaugurated a Certified Angus Beef program to provide the finest beef possible from steaks to prime rib. He has even joined the Angus Breeders Association and sponsors a calf in the calf scramble of the Houston Livestock Show and Rodeo.

With home-style foods and service, Hendee has tried to recreate the feeling of a friendly old-time family restaurant. His whole family is involved (when she was 3, their youngest daughter once showed a couple to a table and gave them menus).

"Our best award is repeat business and we have one of the highest rates of repeat business of any restaurant in Houston," Hendee says.

The casual, homey feeling of a Texas ranch is created with weathered brick, rustic stone fireplaces with wild game trophies, a stuffed armadillo, beamed ceilings, skylights, wood and brass, ceiling fans and hanging ivy and plants. Hendee's wife Nina did the decorative stained glass plaques and found the huge quilt used as a wall hanging in a recently added dining room.

They have developed their own menu, and several items were adapted from Hendee's or employees' families' recipes, such as Ma Maw's Apple Butter and home-baked breads. If there were one flavor associated with Taste of Texas it would be cinnamon. Among their most popular specialties are cinnamon ice cream dessert drinks, cinnamon-flavored coffee and the cinnamony apple butter.

Star Attractions

★ Certified Angus Beef steaks and prime rib. "It's excellent or it's free," says Edd Hendee. As a further guarantee, a framed certificate of deposit for $1,000 hangs on one wall; Hendee says he will give it to anyone who finds a better steak of comparable quality and price.

★ Steaks sold by the ounce; price includes full meal of salad bar, cheese block, homemade bread and one side order. The minimum steak weight is 10 ounces, the size necessary to get the proper thickness for optimum cooking quality, Hendee says. He recommends a 12-ounce minimum for best flavor. There is no charge for splitting the steak among 2 or 3 people. Steaks served sizzling with butter or lemon pepper seasoning.

★ The angus steak sandwich, a charbroiled slice of ribeye on toasted homemade bread. A good choice for those who want a lighter meal or smaller portion of beef.

★ An excellent wine list, particularly strong in California wines. Premium wines by the glass.

★ Coffee made from Colombian beans freshly ground on the premises. Complimentary Cinnamon Coffee served after the meal.

★ Drink specialties such as the Texas Style Margarita, Grand Gold Margarita, Amaretto Freeze and Frozen Pina Colada.

★ Three large television screens in the club for satellite reception of sports events. Special parties for play-off games. Taste of Texas was the first restaurant to sign a TV satellite agreement to show the Houston Rockets professional basketball games.

★ Newsletter sent periodically to about 9,000 customers on the mailing list. It includes news about restaurant events, new menu items and recipes.

★ Personal response to many diners who fill out comment cards.

★ The Ambassador Pass, a gift certificate for a free meal. Included in the newsletter twice a year and occasionally sent to customers in response to their comments on comment cards.

Taste of Texas Cornbread

3   eggs
2   cups water
3   cups cornbread mix
2   tablespoons sugar
1   (15-ounce) can cream-style corn
2   to 4 ounces chopped jalapenos (seeded and ribs removed) or 1 (4-ounce) can green chilies, chopped

Lightly grease a 13x9x2-inch pan. Preheat oven to 425 degrees or 400 degrees if using ovenproof glass pan.

Beat eggs slightly in bowl. Add water, cornbread mix and sugar.

Add corn and jalapenos and stir just until well blended.

Pour into prepared pan and bake 30 to 35 minutes at 425 degrees, or until cornbread springs back when touched in the middle.

Remove from oven and let cool a few minutes before cutting.

Serves 12 to 15.

Note: This is lower in calories than many similar recipes because it calls for no oil, sour cream or milk, yet it has a moist texture. If desired, add 1 large grated onion.

Tortilla Soup

1½ onions, diced
1½ teaspoons garlic powder
1 ounce chopped jalapenos
½ stick (4 tablespoons) margarine
3 cups tomato juice
1 teaspoon black pepper
¼ cup picante sauce
1½ quarts beef bouillon or stock
1 to 2 tablespoons chili (without beans)
    Corn tortilla chips
    Grated yellow cheese

Saute onion, half the garlic powder and jalapenos in margarine until onion is transparent.

Combine tomato juice, pepper, picante sauce and remaining garlic powder.

When onions are sauteed, add beef bouillon and chili. Simmer 15 minutes.

To serve: place 4 crushed tortilla chips and 1 to 2 tablespoons grated cheese in bottom of each bowl; pour soup over. Add a few fresh chips on top.

Serves 8.

Mushrooms in Butter

2 pounds fresh mushrooms
½ stick (4 tablespoons) butter or margarine
½ yellow onion, diced
1 garlic clove, chopped
2 ounces Chablis or other dry white wine
1 cup beef broth
½ cup chicken broth
    Pinch of salt (optional)

Wash mushrooms gently, pat dry and slice. Melt butter in large saucepan, add onion and garlic and saute until browned.

Reduce heat and add wine, broth and salt to taste.

Add mushrooms and simmer over low heat 10 to 15 minutes. Turn heat off and cool about 20 minutes.

Serves 8 as a side dish.

Sizzling Butter Sauce

1 pound butter, clarified
1 teaspoon granulated garlic (or 1 clove, mashed)
    Juice of 1 lemon

To clarify butter, melt, skim off foam and pour clear butter off the sediment at the bottom of pan into another pan.

Add garlic, squeeze lemon juice into butter and stir.

Pour over steaks (at Taste of Texas, butter is poured over steaks on a sizzling platter heated to 300 degrees.)

Cinnamon Coffee

Edd Hendee says he "stole" this recipe from a restaurant at Disney World. However it was acquired, customers are glad he introduced this after-dinner coffee to Houston. It has a rich, intriguing what-is-it? taste.

3   **ounces freshly ground Colombian coffee**
3   **tablespoons ground cinnamon**
4   **cinnamon sticks**
4   **heaping teaspoons brown sugar**

Place coffee grounds in coffeemaker brew basket. Top with ground cinnamon.

Add cinnamon sticks to the pot with brown sugar.

Brew coffee and let steep 15 minutes.

Makes 12 cups.

Cinnamon Slammer

½   **ounce amaretto liqueur**
½   **ounce hazelnut liqueur (Frangelico)**
½   **ounce white creme de cacao**
4   **scoops cinnamon ice cream***

Combine liqueurs and ice cream in electric blender and mix until milkshake consistency.

Makes 1.

*If cinnamon ice cream is not available, mix 2 tablespoons ground cinnamon into 1 quart softened vanilla ice cream. Refreeze to let flavors blend, if desired.

Serve as dessert drink.

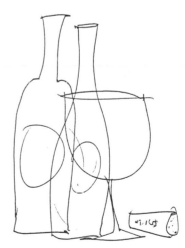

Taste of Texas
90 Town & Country Village on Memorial
Houston, 77024
932-6901

Tila's

FAVORITES

Gazpacho

*Spicy Blue Cornmeal Gulf Shrimp
with Cold Marinated Tomatoes*

Chicken Torta Sandwich

Refried Black Beans

Sauteed Bananas Flamed in Dark Rum

Tila's is one of Houston's leading lights in creative cuisine. Owner/chef Clive Duval is behind the eclectic menu of specialties with a Latin flair.

Duval has received national recognition in newspapers, food magazines, cookbooks and television and is one of the chefs featured in the public television series on "Creative Chefs of the Southwest."

After living and traveling in Central and Latin America, he was inspired to develop his Creative Latin Cuisine. He explores the culinary world beyond Mexico, drawing from Latin America, South America and the American Southwest.

Duval had a checkered career before entering the restaurant business here in 1982. The son of a Virginia state senator, he attended college in the States and a Presbyterian seminary in England. For four years, he operated farms for lemon grass and soy beans and a silver mine in Central America. He returned to the U.S. and worked in a friend's restaurant in Chattanooga. That experience persuaded him to enroll in the Philadelphia Restaurant School.

He jogs, skis and is an enthusiastic mountain climber (in 1986 he scaled Mount McKinley, the highest peak in North America.)

Another Tila's is scheduled to open in Washington, D.C., in 1987.

★ An eclectic menu that keeps customers coming back "to see what Clive is doing this week". It changes constantly as Duval refines and perfects each dish and searches for exciting new tastes. Today it might be a salsa sparked with avocado, tamarind, roasted chilies or pumpkin seeds; tomorrow, China-Latina wontons (sauteed egg rolls stuffed with deviled shrimp) or enchiladas of grilled steak in blue corn tortillas.

★ Menus starred to indicate lighter fare such as Tortilla Soup, charcoal roasted half chicken or chicken breast marinated in citrus juices, fresh grilled swordfish and smoked shrimp salad.

★ A menu of little meals (Comidas Pequenas) or snacks such as stuffed chilies with pico de gallo and black beans, quesadillas, tortas (layered sandwiches of grilled chicken breast, steak or roast pork) and grilled tacos.

★ Taste comes first, but many dishes are modified to use less fat and more healthful ingredients. Fat is routinely trimmed from the bacon used in the bean soup and from chicken, less cream is used than in authentic recipes and some dishes are made with part skim milk cheeses. On request, most chicken dishes can be prepared with skinned chicken breast.

★ Lively, casual setting. Particularly noteworthy are collector-quality signed prints by a Japanese artist, Nakian, and posters in soft rainbow colors by Gallagher, Paul Jenkins and Peter Kitchell.

★ Patio that seats 30 with terra cotta fountain, gas lights and music.

★ Good selection of beers including popular imported Mexican light and dark beers.

★ Catering and carry-out (orders to go encouraged).

Tila's Gazpacho

6 tomatoes, roasted, peeled and seeded
¼ cup chicken stock
4 cups cocktail vegetable juice
1 green onion, chopped
1 garlic clove, minced
1 small poblano chile
1 small cucumber, peeled, seeded and chopped
1 small carrot, finely diced
½ red bell pepper, chopped
1 small zucchini, chopped
  Kernels from 1 ear corn
¼ cantaloupe, peeled and chopped
¼ cup freshly squeezed lime juice
¼ cup vermouth
2 tablespoons olive oil
  Freshly ground black pepper, salt, basil and tarragon to taste
  Fried corn tortilla strips and chopped avocado for garnish

Roast tomatoes on flat griddle or in skillet over high heat until black and blistered on all sides. At Tila's, everything is roasted over hot charcoal mesquite, which imparts a special smoky flavor.

Place 4 tomatoes in blender or food processor with chicken stock and vegetable juice. Puree and pour into large mixing bowl.

Stir in remaining chopped tomatoes, onion, garlic, chile, cucumber, carrot, bell pepper, zucchini, corn and cantaloupe.

Add lime juice, vermouth and olive oil; season to taste with fresh herbs. Refrigerate 2 hours. Serve garnished with a handful of fried tortilla strips and some chopped avocado.

To prepare tortillas: Cut corn tortillas into strips with kitchen scissors. Saute in hot oil until coffee colored. Pat dry with paper towels.

Serves 8 to 10

Spicy Blue Cornmeal Gulf Shrimp With Cold Marinated Tomatoes

4 ripe tomatoes, peeled and cut in wedges
  Tila's Special Marinade (recipe follows)
1 pound (8- to 12-count) fresh Gulf shrimp
  Fresh parsley and chervil leaves
  Cayenne
  Cavender's Greek Seasoning or other seasoned salt mixture
  Blue cornmeal for dredging
3 tablespoons olive oil
  All-purpose flour for dredging
  Water
¼ cup grated Fontina cheese
⅛ cup grated Gorgonzola cheese
⅛ cup ricotta cheese
  Paprika and chives for garnish

Marinate tomatoes according to recipe that follows. Combine herbs and spices with blue cornmeal.

Heat olive oil in saute pan until smoking. Roll shrimp in flour, dip in water and roll in seasoned cornmeal. Saute shrimp until golden, remove and drain on paper towels.

Remove tomatoes from marinade with slotted spoon and gently press out marinade. Toss with sauteed shrimp. Place in ovenproof casserole. Combine the three cheeses and sprinkle over top of shrimp and tomatoes.

Place under broiler until cheese is melted. Garnish with paprika and chives. Serve with hot flour tortillas.

Serves 4 as an appetizer.

Tila's Special Marinade
1 teaspoon brown sugar
1 green onion, chopped
1 teaspoon cracked black pepper
½ teaspoon celery salt
¼ teaspoon allspice
1 teaspoon Dijon mustard
½ cup red rice wine vinegar
½ cup olive oil

Combine sugar, onion, spices and mustard in a bowl with vinegar. Slowly whisk in oil until fully incorporated.

Pour over tomatoes and let marinate at room temperature 30 minutes. Makes 1 cup.

Chicken Torta

Marinade for Torta (recipe follows)
1 chicken breast, boned, marinated and grilled
Tila's Basting Sauce
1 (10-inch) French roll
1 tablespoon olive oil
4 tablespoons grated Muenster cheese
3 tablespoons Refried Black Beans (recipe follows)
½ cup chopped lettuce
2 tablespoons diced tomatoes
2 tablespoons diced white onion
4 slices Haas avocado
4 slices pickled jalapenos
1 tablespoon sour cream

Prepare marinade. Marinate chicken breast 1 hour. Cook over charcoal grill about 4 to 5 minutes on each side over white-hot coals. Baste with Tila's Basting Sauce.

Cut bread in half lengthwise. Cut off rounded part of outer crust, both top and bottom, and the pointed ends. Brush each side with oil.

Brown on grill on both sides. Remove from grill and layer half the following ingredients in order: cheese, black beans, meat.

On the other half, in order, place: lettuce, tomatoes, onion, avocado slices and jalapenos. Garnish with sour cream. Makes 1 sandwich.

Marinade For Torta
3 tablespoons barbecue sauce
1 tablespoon finely minced fresh ginger
½ cup fresh, chopped pineapple
½ cup orange juice
Juice of 1 Persian lime
1 tablespoon cracked black pepper
1 teaspoon Kosher salt
¼ cup safflower oil
10 leaves fresh mint, chopped

Combine all ingredients and pour over chicken. Refrigerate 1 hour, uncovered.

Tila's Basting Sauce
3 cups fresh chicken stock
⅛ pound unsalted butter
Juice of 2 oranges
1 orange, thinly sliced
Juice of 3 Persian limes
2 tablespoons cracked black pepper
3 garlic cloves, minced
1 small white onion, thinly sliced

Combine all ingredients and use as basting sauce for any grilled meat.

Refried Black Beans

1   pound dried black beans
2   small white onions
2   garlic cloves
2   cups chicken stock
½   pound bacon
3   jalapenos
    Salt and white pepper to taste
3   tablespoons safflower oil
¾   pound grated white Cheddar or feta
    cheese
3   green onions

Wash beans thoroughly; pick over carefully and remove any stones. Place in stockpot with water to cover by at least 3 inches. Cover pot and bring to a boil. Skim off foam periodically if necessary. Reduce heat to a steady simmer and partially remove lid. Simmer about 1 hour.

Quarter and add 1 onion with garlic cloves and chicken stock. Continue simmering 1 hour, skimming off foam. The beans should be very tender, splitting apart at the seams.

Mince bacon and chop jalapenos and remaining onion. Saute bacon until crisp and almost burnt; pour off rendered fat, reserving 3 to 4 tablespoons. Saute chopped onion and jalapenos in bacon fat until onion is translucent.

When beans are tender, drain off liquid and reserve. Let cool for a few minutes. Place beans in blender with 3 to 4 cups of the reserved liquid.

Add sauteed bacon, onion and jalapenos, any remaining bacon fat and salt and pepper to taste. Puree to a thick, but still chunky, consistency. Depending on the size of the blender, you have have to do this in several batches.

Heat oil in saute pan. Return beans to pan and cook until most of the liquid is evaporated, about 5 to 10 minutes.

Stir constantly because cooked black beans burn easily. Sprinkle with grated cheese and green onion just before serving.

Serves 6

Sauteed Bananas Flamed in Dark Rum

1   large ripe banana
⅛   pound unsalted butter
¼   cup dark rum
1   teaspoon allspice
1   heaping tablespoon brown sugar
¼   cup orange juice
⅛   cup lime juice
    Vanilla bean ice cream (Tila's uses
    Blue Bell)

Peel and split banana lengthwise. Melt butter in skillet. Add banana slices and saute until butter turns coffee-colored and banana begins to soften.

Deglaze with rum (pour rum into pan and scrape up cooking bits from bottom). Add allspice, brown sugar and juices. Simmer over low heat 1 minute.

Remove banana to serving plate. Top with large scoop of ice cream. Continue to simmer sauce 1 to 2 minutes longer, or until it thickly coats the back of a spoon.

Flame carefully (can use a long taper match) and quickly pour over ice cream.

Note: This is a flavorful, but not sweet dessert.

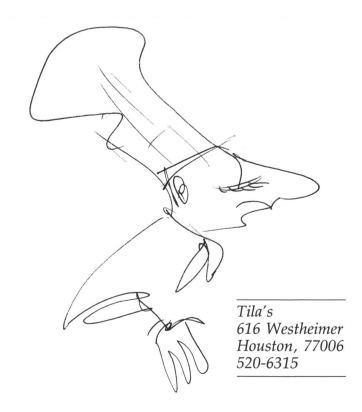

Tila's
616 Westheimer
Houston, 77006
520-6315

Special helps

Some terms and recipes from restaurant owners and professional chefs may be unfamiliar to the home cook. Here are several that you may see frequently.

Bearnaise Sauce — A classic French egg-butter sauce which takes its name from Bearn, a French province in the Pyrenees. It is made with wine, vinegar, tarragon and shallots and resembles hollandaise in consistency.

1	teaspoon chopped shallots
1	sprig each fresh tarragon and chervil, coarsely chopped
2	peppercorns
	Dash of salt
¼	cup tarragon vinegar
5	egg yolks
¾	cup melted butter
	Pinch of cayenne

In saucepan, simmer shallots, tarragon and chervil, peppercorns, salt and vinegar over low heat until vinegar is reduced by two-thirds. Cool to lukewarm. Remove peppercorns.

Beat egg yolks with wire whisk. Place pan over low heat. Add butter gradually, whisking constantly until sauce thickens. Add cayenne. Serve immediately or keep warm in covered container placed in hot water (such as double boiler).

The sauce is easier if made in blender, but use no more than 3 eggs: Combine ¼ cup white wine and 2 tablespoons tarragon vinegar, 1 tablespoon chopped shallots, 2 peppercorns and 1 sprig each minced fresh tarragon, chervil and parsley. Simmer in saucepan until reduced by half. Cool to lukewarm. Remove peppercorns.

Combine in blender container with 3 egg yolks and a dash of salt. Cover and blend on high for a few seconds, then add ¾ cup melted butter in a gradual, steady stream. When all butter is added, sauce should be smooth and thickened. If not, blend a few seconds longer.

Blue cornmeal — Typical New Mexican ingredient used in Southwestern cooking (see Tila's), blue cornmeal provides distinctive taste and color. Found in a few stores locally (see Shopping Guide) or may be ordered from Williams-Sonoma.

Capers — the small green berry-like buds of the caper bush used as a condiment or to give piquant flavor to sauces (see Snapper Veracruzana from San Carlos). Usually available bottled or pickled in vinegar.

Clarified butter — Often used in delicate, fine dishes because it doesn't burn as easily as whole butter. Melt butter (preferably unsalted) over low heat until the foam disappears from top and sediment collects in pan. Butter should be golden yellow and clear; do not let burn. Pour clear butter off; discard sediment.

Cream — When chefs talk about cream, they usually mean heavy cream which is generally labeled whipping cream in this part of the country. When whipped, it doubles in volume. Most whipping cream now is ultra-pasteurized for longer shelf life. Better texture and optimum volume are achieved if the cream, bowl and beaters are thoroughly chilled before the cream is beaten. Better supermarkets sometimes stock cream labeled heavy whipping cream.

If light cream is specified, look for cream labeled coffee cream (or occasionally, table cream).

Deglaze — Pour off all but a tablespoon or two of accumulated fat from sauteed food. Add stock, water, wine or liquid called for in the recipe and simmer, scraping up browned bits from bottom of pan with a wooden spoon.

Diet alert — Low-fat cheeses, non-fat yogurt, skim milk and evaporated skim milk, egg substitute, light cream cheese, light mayonnaise and salad dressing and soft tub margarine and diet margarine may often be substituted for higher fat, higher calorie ingredients without markedly affecting taste.

Substitutions have been suggested in many recipes. In others, which are obviously high-fat or high-calorie, substitutions have not been suggested because we felt taste or the integrity of the recipe was affected — or because the indulgence is worth it.

Most medical experts and health organizations currently advocate the 50-30-20 diet — 50 percent of calories from carbohydrate, 30 percent or less from fat and 20 percent from protein.

Carbohydrates should be complex carbohydrates such as fresh vegetables, fruits, grains and beans, not refined carbohydrates. Recommended fat guidelines are that 10 percent should come from polyunsaturated fat, less than 10 percent from saturated fat and the rest from monounsaturated fats such as olive oil.

Check labels carefully for nutritional analysis of products.

Herbs — Fresh are preferable if of good quality. They are increasingly easier to find in Houston supermarkets. The rule of thumb in substituting dried herbs is one to three — one teaspoon dried substituted for three teaspoons fresh.

Olive oil — Extra virgin olive oil is preferred by most chefs because it is the finest quality and has a more delicate flavor. Because it has a low smoking point, it is not suitable for frying as are lower grades. Use extra virgin olive oil for salad dressings or uncooked dishes.

Less expensive grades such as superfine virgin, virgin or those labeled "pure" are better for everyday use. Store all olive oil in a cool, dark place.

Pasta — Make your own or purchase from pasta shops; use fresh or dried. Fresh pasta is best with light, fresh tomato sauces or delicate cream sauces; dried pasta, with heartier long-simmered meat and red sauces.

Fresh pasta takes only 3 to 5 minutes to cook; dried may take as long as 15. Pasta should always be cooked "al dente" which means "firm to the tooth". It should lose its floury taste, but not be hard or mushy. Do not rinse cooked pasta with cold water unless using pasta for salads.

Peppers — To roast bell peppers, rinse and dry, place on baking sheet and broil 4 to 5 inches from heat 5 minutes on each side or until the surface of each pepper is blistered and somewhat blackened. Place in plastic bag, seal and let steam 15 to 20 minutes. Remove from bag and rub or scrape off peel (skins should peel off easily).

Other methods: Rub peppers with oil (optional) and grill over mesquite or charcoal, or place on end of long-tined fork and hold over gas burner until charred. Proceed as above to peel.

Handle jalapenos and other hot peppers with care as peppers and fumes can irritate skin and eyes. Removing the walls and seeds cuts the heat.

Ricotta salata (called for in the Arugula Salad With Stuffed Peppers from Damian's) — A salted, drained ricotta cheese. Available in select supermarkets, cheese shops and some gourmet shops.

Roux — A mixture of flour and fat that is the thickening base for many sauces and soups, particularly Cajun dishes such as gumbo. The usual method is to heat oil until it is at the point of smoking, then to whisk in flour and stir constantly until mixture is a dark mahogany brown, almost black. Roux requires a lot of attention; it must be stirred or whisked almost constantly for 45 minutes to an hour or it will burn.

Roux is much easier in the microwave. The following method is described by newspaper microwave columnists Ann Steiner and CiCi Williamson in their first book, "Microwave Know-How."

Heat ½ cup each oil and flour in a 4-cup glass measure. Microwave on high power 6 to 7 minutes, stirring every minute after 4 minutes, until a deep brown roux is formed.

Stock — Stocks made on the premises is the rule with chefs of restaurants represented in this book, but most realize that busy home cooks will use canned broth and stocks. Unfortunately, canned broths tend to be too salty so choose good quality canned products and adjust salt called for in the recipe.

When making stock at home, use a non-aluminum pan. For clear stock, skim foam and scum off top as it accumulates. Stir as little as possible to prevent clouding. Stock should simmer slowly, not boil. Cool quickly (setting the pan of stock in a container or sink or cold water speeds the process). Chill, then remove congealed fat from top. Refrigerate or freeze.

Beef stock: Combine 2 to 4 pounds beef bones and meaty soup bones and trimmings (brown half the meat) in a saucepot. Add 3 quarts cold water, 8 peppercorns, 1 each onion, carrot and celery rib cut in pieces, 3 whole cloves, 1 bay leaf, 5 sprigs parsley and other desired herbs such as dried thyme. Bring to a boil and skim off foam. Simmer covered 3 hours, skimming occasionally. Strain stock, cool quickly and refrigerate or freeze. When cold, remove any solid fat that has risen to the top. (Remove fat before freezing.)

Chicken stock: Place 3 pounds bony chicken parts in a stockpot with 3 quarts cold water, a quartered onion stuck with 2 whole cloves, 2 each celery ribs and carrots, 10 peppercorns, 5 sprigs parsley and 1 bay leaf. Cover pot, bring to a boil over medium heat, then reduce heat and simmer stock partially covered, 2 to 3 hours. For a clear stock, skim off foam and scum that collects on the surface. Add salt to taste after about 1 hour. Strain stock and discard bones and solids. Let cool. Refrigerate or freeze when cool.

Fish stock: Follow method for chicken stock above using 2 pounds fish bones, heads and tails, half the amount of onion, celery and carrots, 6 peppercorns and 1 cup dry white wine if desired. Fish stock needs to be simmered uncovered only about 30 minutes, until reduced by half. Longer simmering may produce off tastes. Skim while simmering. Let cool uncovered. When cool, refrigerate or freeze.

Balsamic vinegar — A dark, aged Italian vinegar that is very popular with food professionals and the avant garde.

Shopping Guide

Here are some sources for foreign or gourmet ingredients called for in recipes in "Houston Gourmet Cooks."

General

Fiesta Marts, 13 locations; check the Yellow Pages or call 869-5060 for location nearest you. Excellent source for all sorts of fresh and packaged foreign foods, imported items, especially Mexican, Latin, Chinese, Asian and Middle Eastern. Largest market is at Bellaire Boulevard and Hillcroft. Newest location is a 75,000-square-foot store at Bellaire Boulevard and Hwy. 6 which has the ambiance of a Mexican mercado. It features specialty baked goods, carry-out Japanese sushi, fajitas, all kinds of exotic fresh produce.

Jim Jamail and Sons, 3114 Kirby Dr. If Jamail's doesn't have it, it will be hard to find in Houston. Gourmet items, full lines of imported and domestic cheeses, fresh fruits and vegetables, herbs, excellent meats and fish, low-cholesterol, low-sodium items, imported sauces, seasonings and condiments, wines, pastas, chocolates, baked goods, coffees and teas.

Jumbo Supermarkets, 9750 Fondren, 10250 Westheimer and West Columbia, Texas. Good source for Chinese, Asian, Mexican, Middle Eastern and Cajun ingredients including fresh produce and sauces.

Whole Foods Market, 2900 S. Shepherd. Imported and/or organically grown fruits and vegetables, sauces, condiments, wide variety of bulk spices and seasonings, cheeses, natural yogurts, frozen foods, additive-free beef and chicken, baked goods, grains, wines, beers, teas, coffees.

Williams-Sonoma, 4076 Westheimer (622-4161) and 30 Town & Country center (465-4775). Sauces, condiments, blue cornmeal, own line of dry spices, Anaheim chilies, Martelli pasta, professional vanilla, Callebaut and confiture chocolate (white, chips and dipping chocolate).

Chinese, Asian

Various markets in Chinatown east of Main Street around McKinney and St. Emanuel.

Asiatic Import Company, 909 Chartres (227-7979).

Chinatown Market, 1806 Polk Ave. (650-0757).

Diho Market, 9280 Bellaire Blvd. (988-1881). Extensive stock of Chinese and Oriental products, fresh meats, fish, wines, sauces, frozen and prepared items.

Dynasty Supermarket in Dynasty Plaza, 9600 Bellaire (995-4088). Full line supermarket of Oriental and Chinese staples, condiments and hot deli items; fresh fish, wines and beers.

Korea Super Market, 6427 Bissonnet, 772-6160.

Daido Japanese Market, Westheimer at Wilcrest (785-0815).

Indian

Jay Stores, 6688 Southwest Fwy.

Patel Brothers, 6822 Harwin.

Both have a full line of Indian ingredients and products, spices and condiments; some Asian products.

Vietnamese

Saigon Supermarket, 10815 Beechnut at Wilcrest.

Crystal Palace on Milam.

Hoa Nam, 8282 Bellaire.

Vietnam Plaza, 2200 Jefferson, 222-6280.

Viet Hoa Supermarket, 8200 Wilcrest at Beechnut, 561-8706.

Index

APPETIZERS
Caponata (Damian's) 25
Ceviche (Sausalito) 91
Crab Royal with House Dressing (The Lancaster Grille) 31
Crostini Fried Sandwich (Montesano Ristorante Italiano) 53
Mussels, Steamed (Nash D'Amico's Pasta & Clam Bar) 57
Redfish Fritters with Jalapeno Tartar Sauce (Brennan's) 19
Red Spanish Shrimp (Montesano Ristorante Italiano) 52
Salmon Mousse Mold (Backstreet Cafe) 11
Saute Crabmeat Marlene (Lantern Inn) 35
Scallops Provencale (La Tour d'Argent) 43
Sopes (San Carlos) 87
Spicy Blue Cornmeal Gulf Shrimp with Cold Marinated Tomatoes (Tila's) 99
Squid, Fried (Nash D'Amico's Pasta & Clam Bar) 57
Wild Mushroom Raviolis with Chive Sauce (La Reserve) 39

BEVERAGES
Cinnamon Coffee (Taste of Texas) 97
Cinnamon Slammer (Taste of Texas) 97

BREADS
Hot Cakes (Oak'n Bucket) 65
Taste of Texas Cornbread 95

CHICKEN AND POULTRY
Baked Duck with Rice Dressing (Magnolia Bar & Grill) 49
Black Pepper Pasta with Sweet Garlic Cream and Chicken (Ruggles Grill) 84
Breast of Chicken (Oak'n Bucket) 66
Breast of Cornish Hen (Lantern Inn) 35
Chicken Breast a la Grecque (Sausalito) 92
Chicken Dick (Bayou City Oyster Company) 16
Chicken Parmesan (Nash D'Amico's Pasta & Clam Bar) 58
Chicken Torta (Tila's) 100
Chilaquiles (San Carlos) 88
General Tso's Chicken (Peng's) 75
Grilled Chicken Sandwich (Backstreet Cafe) 12
Grilled Shrimp and Chicken on Brochette (Rotisserie for Beef and Bird) 80
Josef's Chicken Salad (Damian's) 26
Warm Grilled Chicken Salad with Roquefort and Walnuts (Ruggles Grill) 84

DESSERTS
Bananas, Sauteed and Flamed in Dark Rum (Tila's) 101
Chocolate Dutchman Flambe (Lantern Inn) 37
Cinnamon Slammer (Taste of Texas) 97
Creole Bread Pudding Souffle with Whiskey Sauce (Brennan's) 23
French Silk Chocolate Pie (Oak'n Bucket) 67
Hot Apple Tart with Pastry Cream and Apricot Sauce (La Tour d'Argent) 45
Lemon Ice Cream (Bayou City Oyster Company) 17
Mango Mousse (San Carlos) 89
Meringue Tartlettes with Raspberries (La Reserve) 41

Negre en Chemise (Ouisie's) 73
Oranges Marissa (Damian's) 29
Pears, Fresh Poached with Zabaglione Sauce (Rotisserie for Beef and Bird) . . . 81
Pina Teocali (Ninfa's) 63
Tiramisu (Montesano Ristorante Italiano) 55
White Chocolate Mousse (The Lancaster Grille) 33
White Chocolate Mousse (Magnolia Bar & Grill) 49

Cakes
    Blanca's Strawberry Cream Roll (Ruggles Grill) 85
    Carrot Cake (Backstreet Cafe) 13
    Chocolate Amaretto Cheesecake (Backstreet Cafe) 13
    Domenico's Cheesecake (Sausalito) 93

FISH AND SEAFOOD

Ceviche (Sausalito) 91
Clear Vegetable Soup with Seafood (La Tour d'Argent) 44

Crab
    Crab Royal with House Dressing (The Lancaster Grille) 31
    Saute Crabmeat Marlene (Lantern Inn) 35
    Snapper and Crab Chowder (Ruggles Grill) 83
    Zucchini Bisque with Crabmeat (La Reserve) 40

Crawfish
    Crawfish Bisque/Stuffed Shells (Magnolia Bar & Grill) 47
    Crawfish Enchiladas (Brennan's) 20
    Crawfish Etouffee (Magnolia Bar & Grill) 47
    Crawfish Salsa with Grilled Red Snapper (Ruggles Grill) 85
Fish Milano Flambe (Lantern Inn) 37
Linguine and Fresh Seafood in a Spicy Sauce (Rotisserie) 79
Mussels, Steamed (Nash D'Amico's Pasta & Clam Bar) 57

Redfish
    Redfish Aldo (Sausalito) 92
    Redfish Fritters with Jalapeno Tartar Sauce (Brennan's) 19

Red Snapper
    Fish Milano Flambe (Lantern Inn) 37
    Grilled Red Snapper with Spicy Crawfish Salsa (Ruggles Grill) 85
    Snapper and Crab Chowder (Ruggles Grill) 83
    Snapper Royale (Bayou City Oyster Company) 15
    Snapper Russo (Damian's) 27
    Snapper Veracruzana (San Carlos) 88

Salmon
    Poached Salmon with Green Sauce (The Lancaster Grille) 32
    Salmon Mousse Mold (Backstreet Cafe) 11
Scallops Provencale (La Tour d'Argent) 43
Seafood Casserole (Bayou City Oyster Company) 15
Seafood Gumbo (Backstreet Cafe) 11
Seafood Stuffed Eggplant (Magnolia Bar & Grill) 48

Shrimp
    Divinity Shrimp (Bayou City Oyster Company) 16
    Grilled Shrimp and Chicken on Brochette (Rotisserie for Beef and Bird) . . . 80
    Red Spanish Shrimp (Montesano Ristorante Italiano) 52
    Shrimp Acapulco (Ouisie's) 69
    Spicy Blue Cornmeal Gulf Shrimp with Cold Marinated Tomatoes (Tila's) . . 99
Squid, Fried (Nash D'Amico's Pasta & Clam Bar) 57
Trout with Roasted Pecans/Creole Meuniere Sauce (Brennan's) 21
Tuna, Grilled with Gremalotta (Ouisie's) 69

MEAT
Beef
    Beef Tenderloin with Two Sauces (La Reserve) 40
    Fajitas/Marinated Onions with Pico de Gallo (Ninfa's) 61
    Special Beef (Peng's) 76
    Steak Diane for Two (Lantern Inn) 36
    Tournedos a la Maison (The Lancaster Grille) 32
Lamb
    Lamb Chili (Brennan's) 22
    Lamb Loin with Spinach Cakes (La Reserve) 41
    Lamb Medallions with Basil Sauce (La Tour d'Argent) 44
Veal
    Medallions of Veal with Julienne of Vegetables and Cheese (Rotisserie for Beef and Bird) . 80
    Veal Cutlet Milanese (Montesano Ristorante Italiano) 53
Stuffed Pork Tenders (Ouisie's) 70

PASTA/RICE
Black Pepper Pasta with Sweet Garlic Cream and Chicken (Ruggles Grill) 84
Fettucine Dino (Sausalito) 92
Fried Noodles with 10 Ingredients (Peng's) 77
Linguine and Fresh Seafood in a Spicy Sauce (Rotisserie for Beef and Bird) 79
Perciatelli Pasta Roma (Montesano Ristorante Italiano) 54
Spinach Pasta (Nash D'Amico's Pasta & Clam Bar) 59
Tortellini in Brodo (Damian's) 28
Rice
    Lemon Ginger Rice/Vegetarian Variation (Ouisie's) 72
    Mexican Rice (Ninfa's) 63
    Rice Dressing with Baked Duck (Magnolia Bar & Grill) 49

SALADS/SALAD DRESSINGS
Arugula Salad with Stuffed Peppers (Damian's) 26
Bammel Garden Salad with Goat Cheese (Sausalito) 91
Bibb Lettuce and Stilton Salad with House Dressing (The Lancaster Grille) 33
Chicken
    Chicken and Broccoli Salad (Backstreet Cafe) 12
    Josef's Chicken Salad with Mayonnaise (Damian's) 26
    Warm Grilled Chicken Salad with Roquefort and Walnuts/Dressing (Ruggles Grill) 84
House Salad with Mayonnaise Dressing (Nash D'Amico's Pasta & Clam Bar) 58
Magnolia Salad Dressing/Seafood Salad (Magnolia Bar & Grill) 48
Salade Panachee/Olive Oil Vinaigrette (La Tour d'Argent) 43

SANDWICHES
Chicken Torta/Marinade/Basting Sauce (Tila's) 100
Crostini Fried Sandwich (Montesano Ristorante Italiano) 53
Grilled Chicken Sandwich with Honey Mustard Dressing (Backstreet Cafe) 12
Roasted Red Bell Peppers with Bacon and Cheese Sandwich (Ouisie's) 71

SAUCES, MARINADES, SEASONINGS
Apricot Sauce, with Hot Apple Tart, Pastry Cream (La Tour d'Argent) 45
Basil Butter, Garlic Butter (La Tour d'Argent) 43
Beurre Blanc, with Grilled Red Snapper with Spicy Crawfish Salsa (Ruggles Grill) . . . 85
Creole Meuniere Sauce, with Trout with Roasted Pecans (Brennan's) 21
Creole Seafood Seasoning, with Trout with Roasted Pecans (Brennan's) 21
Grain Mustard Sauce, with Beef Tenderloin (La Reserve) 40
Green Chili Salsa, with Crawfish Enchiladas (Brennan's) 20
Green Sauce, with Poached Salmon (The Lancaster Grille) 32

Green Sauce (Ninfa's) 62
Gremalotta, with Grilled Tuna (Ouisie's) 69
Horseradish Dipping Sauce, with Fried Mushrooms (Oak'n Bucket) 66
Horseradish Sauce, with Beef Tenderloin (La Reserve) 40
Jalapeno Tartar Sauce, with Redfish Fritters (Brennan's) 19
Marinade and Basting Sauce for Chicken Torta (Tila's) 100
Marinade for Grilled Shrimp and Chicken (Rotisserie for Beef and Bird) 80
Marinara Sauce (Nash D'Amico's Pasta & Clam Bar) 59
Pico de Gallo (Ninfa's) 61
Pico de Gallo, with Shrimp Acapulco (Ouisie's) 69
Raspberry Sauce, with Meringue Tartlettes (La Reserve) 41
Sizzling Butter Sauce for steak (Taste of Texas) 96
Spicy Crawfish Salsa and Spicy Oil, with Grilled Red Snapper (Ruggles Grill) . 85
Tila's Special Marinade for Spicy Blue Cornmeal Shrimp 99
Whiskey Sauce with Creole Bread Pudding Souffle (Brennan's) 23
Zabaglione Sauce/Poached Fresh Pears (Rotisserie for Beef and Bird) 81

SOUP
Bisque of Butternut Squash and Apples (Rotisserie for Beef and Bird) 79
Cheese Soup (Oak'n Bucket) 65
Clear Vegetable Soup with Seafood (La Tour d'Argent) 44
Crawfish Bisque/Stuffed Shells (Magnolia Bar & Grill) 47
Cream of Onion Soup (The Lancaster Grille) 31
Gazpacho (Tila's) 99
New England Clam Chowder (Nash D'Amico's Pasta & Clam Bar) 57
Seafood Gumbo (Backstreet Cafe) 11
Snapper and Crab Chowder (Ruggles Grill) 83
Tortellini in Brodo (Damian's) 28
Tortilla Soup (San Carlos) 87
Tortilla Soup (Taste of Texas) 96
Zucchini Bisque with Crabmeat (La Reserve) 40

VEGETABLES
Creamed Romaine Lettuce (Lantern Inn) 36
Eggplant
    Eggplant Della Mamma (Montesano Ristorante Italiano) 51
    Eggplant in Garlic Sauce (Peng's) 76
    Seafood Stuffed Eggplant (Magnolia Bar & Grill) 48
Mushrooms
    Fried Mushrooms with Horseradish Dipping Sauce (Oak'n Bucket) 66
    Mushrooms in Butter (Taste of Texas) 96
    Mushrooms Sauteed with Garlic Butter (La Tour d'Argent) 45
    Wild Mushroom Raviolis with Chive Sauce (La Reserve) 39
Onions, Marinated with Fajitas (Ninfa's) 61
Potatoes
    Garlic Mashed Potatoes (Ouisie's) 71
    Lemon Potatoes (Bayou City Oyster Company) 17
Refried Beans (Ninfa's) 62
Refried Black Beans (Tila's) 101
Spinach Cakes, with Lamb Loin (La Reserve) 41
Squash
    Bisque of Butternut Squash and Apples (Rotisserie for Beef and Bird) . 79
    Zucchini Bisque with Crabmeat (La Reserve) 40
    Zucchini Il Mulino (Damian's) 25
Vegetarian Variation #1/Lemon Ginger Rice (Ouisie's) 72

About

Ann Criswell

Ann Criswell, has been food editor of the *Houston Chronicle* since 1966, has written freelance food articles, authored two cookbooks and edited several others.

As food editor of the Chronicle, she contributed most of the recipes in the "Texas the Beautiful Cookbook" published in October, 1986.

She is a member of the Newspaper Food Editors and Writers Association, International Food Media Conference, the Houston Culinary Guild and the Spring, Texas, chapter of the Chaine des Rotisseurs.

In 1987 she was named the first honorary member of the South Texas Dietetic Association and received an award of excellence from the American Heart Association, American Cancer Society and Texas Restaurant Association.

Because of a special interest in wine, she has made several wine tours in Europe and California and has judged Texas wine competitions. She has also judged national cooking contests including the National Beef Cook-Off, National Chicken Cooking Contest and America's Bake-Off.

She is a graduate of Texas Woman's University. Her late husband was a Houston newspaperman and she has a daughter, Catherine, 25, and son, Charles, 23.

Who's Who Houston Gourmet Cooks

1. Ann Criswell – Food Editor Houston Chronicle
2. Tom Lile – Bayou City Oyster Company
3. Josef Rasicci – Damian's Cucina Italiana
4. Sonny Lahham – La Tour D'Argent
5. Carlos Rodriguez – San Carlos
6. Chuck Peng – Peng's
7. Jody Larriviere – Magnolia Bar & Grill
8. Amy Lessing – Tila's
9. Kaspar Donier – Le Reserve - Inn On The Park
10. Hans Rometsch – Sausilito
11. Rick Pirooz – Lantern Inn
12. Ronald Whitman – Lancaster Grille
13. Elouise Cooper – Ouisie's
14. Tracy Vaught – Backstreet Cafe
15. Dick Brennan – Brennan's
16. Ninfa Laurenzo – Ninfa's
17. Nash D'Amico – Nash D'Amico's Pasta & Clam Bar
18. Fran Fauntleroy – Coordinator-Publisher
19. Aldo Grubich – Sausilito